Aldus Science and Technology Series

Metals in the Modern World
A Study in Materials Development

Edward Slade

Aldus Books London

First published in the United Kingdom by
Aldus Books Limited, Aldus House, Fitzroy Square, London, W.1
Printed in Italy by Arnoldo Mondadori, Verona
Distributed in the United Kingdom and the Commonwealth by
W. H. Allen & Company, 43, Essex Street, London, W.C.2
Copyright © Aldus Books Limited, London, 1967

ISBN 0-490-00103-3

Contents

Suggested Reading

A. R. Bailey, *A Textbook of Metallurgy*, Macmillan (London, 1960).

D. Birchon, *Dictionary of Metallurgy*, Newnes (London, 1965).

D. J. O. Brandt, *The Manufacture of Iron and Steel*, English Universities Press (London, 1960).

A. H. Cottrell, *Theoretical Structural Metallurgy*, E. Arnold (London, 1955).

W. H. Dennis, *A Hundred Years of Metallurgy*, Duckworth (London, 1963).

Fiber Composite Materials, American Society of Metals (New York, 1965), Chapman & Hall (London, 1965).

D. Fishlock & K. W. Hards, *New Ways of Working Metals*, Newnes (London, 1965).

N. F. Mott, *Atomic Structure and the Strength of Metals*, Pergamon Press (London, 1956).

C. L. McCable & C. L. Bauer, *Metals, Atoms, and Alloys*, McGraw-Hill (New York, 1964).

Recent Progress in Metal Working (for Institution of Metallurgists), Illiffe (London, 1964).

A. Street & W. Alexander, *Metals in the Service of Man*, Penguin Books (Harmondsworth, Middlesex, Revised edition 1964).

The Structure of Metals—A Modern Conception (for Institution of Metallurgists), Illiffe (London, 1959).

Acknowledgments

Page 8 Weleda Ag; photo Schreiber-Roggenkamp: 12 Copper Development Association, London: 30 Westinghouse Electric International Co.: 45 British Crown Copyright/National Physical Laboratory: 51 Prof. Paolo Lombardi, Societa Metallurgica Italiana: 56 Foto Civilini, Piombino: 69 International Nickel Limited, London: 73 Studio Seven, Glasgow: 80 Italsider, Genova: 84 (Top left) Italsider, Genova (Top right) Fiat Turino (Center left) Mannaione, Firenze; Foto Rinadelli, Firenze (Bottom left) Foto Civilini, Piombino (Bottom right) Morgan Crucible Co. Ltd.: 88 British Iron & Steel Federation: 90 Italsider, Genova; photo Ufficio Studi: 92 Italsider Piombino; Foto Civilini, Piombino: 93 British Iron & Steel Federation: 94 (Top) The Machinery Publishing Company Limited, London (Bottom) International Nickel Limited, London: 96 General Electric Company; photo W. H. Sutton: 106 *Metallurgical Review*, London, courtesy Prof. R. V. Coleman: 116 Martin Company, Denver, Colorado, U.S.A.: 126 National Engineering Laboratory, Glasgow: 138 Associated Electrical Industries Ltd., Rugby, England: 141 Notley Advertising Limited: 143 Hawker Siddeley Dynamics Limited: 145 G. & E. Bradley Ltd.: 146 Dorman Long (Steel) Limited: 149 United Steel Companies: 161 Steel Company of Wales: 162 Cambridge Instrument Company Limited: 171 Casa Editrice G. C. Sansoni, Firenze: 175, 178 Hilger & Watts Ltd.: 180 Italsider, Genova; photo Ufficio Studi: 183 Cambridge Instrument Company Limited: 185 Hilger & Watts Ltd.: 189 Prof. E. W. Müller, Pennsylvania State University, U.S.A./*Scientific American*, June, 1957.

1 The Nature of Metals

Three quarters of the elements in the chemist's periodic table are technically metals; it is not surprising, then, that metals enter into every phase of everyday life, of technology, and of science. The transport of oxygen in the blood of (most) animals depends on the presence of atoms, or more accurately ions, of iron in the hemoglobin molecule. Most important industrial chemical processes involve metals either as reactants or as catalysts. Plant life depends crucially on the presence of trace amounts of certain metallic elements in the soil. Despite the chemical and biological importance of metals, however, we ordinarily value metals for their mechanical, electrical, and thermal properties, and it is with these properties of metals that this book is primarily concerned.

Metals are the mechanical load-bearers *par excellence* of our technology, and they owe this position to their combination of strength with ductility, or workability. They are strong enough to satisfy most of our structural needs; at the same time they are sufficiently plastic that they can be bent, cut, pressed, drawn,

A specimen of native copper ($\times 3$). The crystalline nature of the metal is clearly visible in the geometric forms in the photograph.

hammered, and forged into useful shapes. Strength is such a striking feature of metals, particularly to the user of a metal object, that the importance of the ductility of metals is easily overlooked. We shall not labor this point here, except to suggest that if the ultimate alloy, so strong and hard that it could not be bent or cut and so refractory that it could not be melted, were announced, the news would bring small joy to production engineers, however it might delight designers.

Both the apparent strength of metal and its ductility issue from the same source: The nature of the interatomic forces binding atoms one to another. To understand the operation of these forces, and indeed to give a proper definition of a metal, we must undertake some discussion of the basic structure of matter. In particular, it is necessary to introduce some ideas from the modern study of quantum mechanics to explain the essential peculiarity of the metallic state.

Note that in the preceding paragraph we referred to " the metallic state " rather than simply to metals. Metals, being chemical elements, enter into chemical compounds with other elements and the resulting compounds may show none of the properties we consider characteristic of metals. Common table salt (NaCl), for example, is a compound of sodium, a metal, and chlorine, a nonmetal. We shall use this compound, sodium chloride, as an example of a substance that contrasts directly with the typical metal in many of its physical properties. Therefore, when we speak of the essential characteristics of a metal, we are thinking of the metal in its " metallic " or uncombined form.

The Crystalline Structure of Solids

With the notable exception of glass, almost all the materials we commonly call *solids* exist in well-defined crystalline form—that is, the individual atoms are arranged in a regular, orderly pattern called a *crystal lattice*. Examples of two such patterns, or lattices, are shown in the diagram on the right. In the sodium chloride crystal, the sodium and chlorine atoms (or ions, as we should properly call them, as we shall see directly) occupy alternate sites in a three-dimensional rectangular pattern. In the copper crystal shown there are only copper ions present, of course, and each layer

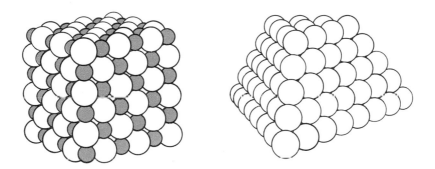

Two simple crystalline forms. On the left, in the crystals of common salt (NaCl), sodium and chlorine ions alternate in a simple rectangular pattern. In the copper crystal (right) the layers are hexagonal, although rectangular planes can also be demonstrated in this crystal.

of copper ions shows a hexagonal pattern. The layers are fitted one on another, like a grocer's display of oranges. Unlike the oranges in the grocer's display, however, the ions in either kind of crystal are held in place by powerful interatomic forces. A considerable mechanical force, or applied stress, would be necessary to derange the structure and to break or deform the crystal.

Enough is known about the forces acting in the crystal to allow us to calculate the mechanical strength of a perfect crystal, either metallic or nonmetallic. This calculation yields a result that is, at first sight, quite astonishing. A perfect crystal of table salt would be as strong as a perfect crystal of most metals. Furthermore, either type of perfect crystal would be many times stronger than the best steel we have so far produced.

The reason practical materials do not show this theoretical strength is that their crystal structure is not perfect. In the first place, real materials—a bar of iron or a lump of rock salt—are not single crystals. They are composed of many individual crystals, usually too small to be seen with the naked eye. (These individual crystals are called *grains* by the metallurgist.) Second, the individual crystals themselves are not perfect, but contain many kinds of irregularities and discontinuities. When we discuss the strength of materials, then, we are less concerned with the strength

Hot-worked copper (×200). The individual grains and the regularity of structure within the grains are clearly visible. In cast material the individual grains would be larger.

Opposite : Schematic representation of atomic structure for hydrogen (H, Z = 1), helium (He, Z = 2), and sodium (Na, Z = 11). The arrangement of electrons into shells will be discussed in the text later.

of perfect crystals than with the effect on this strength of crystalline irregularities, both within and between individual crystals.

Metals differ from typical nonmetals in that metals retain a useful degree of strength in the presence of considerable irregularity in crystal structure. Indeed, certain of these irregularities play an important part in the ductility of metal; they allow the metal crystals to deform smoothly to distribute and so resist an applied load. Further, metal crystals adhere well across grain boundaries (which may, for our present purposes, be considered simply massive irregularities in crystalline structures). We say that metal crystals are *tolerant* of imperfection. By contrast, the typical nonmetallic crystal is intolerant of imperfections. A small irregularity weakens the crystal seriously, and the crystal will not usually deform smoothly under load—it breaks instead. In addition, many nonmetallic crystals hardly adhere across grain boundaries at all.

Why do the two types of crystals behave so differently? On the atomic scale (but not within the nucleus of the atom) the only important basic binding force is the electrostatic attraction between positive and negative electrical charges, and this is true in both metallic and nonmetallic crystals. This attraction (and the corresponding repulsion between charges of like sign) is only the raw material, however, out of which various different kinds of bonds are formed between different kinds of atoms. To see why in the one case the bonds formed are relatively elastic, while in the other case they are equally strong but brittle, we must look more closely at the atom itself, and at the different kinds of atoms.

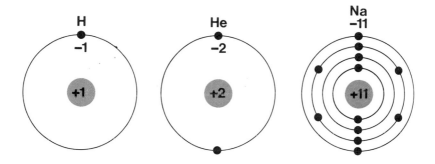

The Structure of Atoms

We think of any atom as a positively charged nucleus surrounded by negatively charged electrons. The positive charge of the nucleus is due to the presence of protons, each of which bears an electrical charge of $+1$. The number of protons in the nucleus is characteristic of the element in question and is called the *atomic number* of the element, usually given the symbol Z. Thus for the simplest element, hydrogen, $Z = 1$; the hydrogen nucleus consists simply of a single proton (usually) and thus the hydrogen nucleus has a total electrical charge of $+1$. The helium nucleus ($Z = 2$) contains 2 protons and so has a positive charge of $+2$—and so on up to lawrencium ($Z = 103$). The number of protons in an atomic nucleus cannot be changed by ordinary chemical means.

An atom is ordinarily provided with sufficient electrons, which each have an electrical charge -1, to balance exactly the electrical charge of the nucleus. Thus in sodium, Na, for which $Z = 11$, the nucleus has a charge of $+11$, and there are normally 11 electrons, each with a charge of -1, so that the whole atom has a total charge of zero; that is, it is normally electrically neutral. Compared to the space over which the electrons range, the nucleus of the atom is small. However, a proton is 1837 times as heavy as an electron, and in all atoms more complex than hydrogen, each proton is accompanied in the nucleus by at least one uncharged particle, called a *neutron*, of mass similar to that of the proton. The bulk of the mass of the atom is thus in the nucleus. (A hydrogen nucleus may contain one or even two neutrons as well as the single proton.)

The protons (and neutrons, if any) are fixed in the nucleus of the atom and, beyond furnishing the positive charge, play no direct role in forming interatomic bonds. The bonds are due to the adventures of the electrons, which may interact with the electrons of other atoms, or even desert one atom altogether and join the electron configuration of an atom of a different element. If this latter event occurs, the two atoms concerned will no longer be electrically neutral, of course. The atom that has lost an electron will now have a total electrical charge of $+1$, since it will have one more proton than it has electrons, and similarly the atom that has gained an electron will have a total electrical charge of -1. These no-longer-neutral atoms would now properly be called *ions*.

The formation of ions leads to one of the simplest types of interatomic bonds. For example, sodium chloride is formed by allowing sodium (Na) to react with chlorine (Cl). Each sodium atom gives up an electron to become a positive ion (Na^+), and the electron is captured by a chlorine atom, which thereby becomes a negative ion (Cl^-). Since the two kinds of ions have opposite electrical charges, they attract each other to form the crystal of sodium chloride, illustrated previously. But we are ahead of our story here, for we.have given no suggestion as to why a sodium atom should so readily give up an electron while a chlorine atom as greedily receives it.

The simplest picture of the atom is one in which the electrons move in orbit around the nucleus, much as the planets move in orbits around the sun. In the atom, the attraction between the positively charged nucleus and the negatively charged electrons replaces the gravitational attraction that holds the planets in their orbits. Actually, it is more to our purpose here to consider the analogy furnished by the artificial earth satellites. As we know, it takes energy to place a satellite in orbit, and the satellite will remain in that orbit only as long as it does not gain or lose energy. If it gains further energy (by restarting its rocket motors in the direction of motion, for example) it will in general move to a higher orbit. If it loses energy (as by grazing the outer layers of the atmosphere, or by firing braking rockets) the orbit will decay and the satellite will eventually tumble back toward the earth.

The same kind of energy considerations apply to the orbits of electrons within atoms. We may think of an electron in a particular orbit as possessing a certain energy; and, other things being equal, an electron of high energy will move in a wider orbit (further from the nucleus, that is) than an electron of lower energy. We must not press the satellite analogy too far, however, for several reasons. In principle we may give the earth satellite any amount of energy we please, and it will find an appropriate orbit. For the electron in the atom, however, only certain discrete orbits are possible, and the energies associated with these different permissible orbits do not vary continuously, but in jumps. The situation is much the same as if we could place earth satellites in orbits at altitudes of exact multiples of 100 miles, but at no altitudes in between. Furthermore, in modern theory it is no longer permissible to think of the electron as a small particle pursuing a definite path within the atom. Rather, we say that the electron can exist only in particular *quantum states* and that certain numbers that describe these quantum states are all we can know about the velocity or position of the electron. For any such quantum state, however, there is, in a given system, a definite energy for the electron, and it is this energy with which we are primarily concerned.

Electron Quantum States

We shall not trouble the reader with the detailed meaning and interrelationships of the four quantum numbers that describe the state of an electron in an atom, but certain basic facts are essential to our argument:

(1) A quantum state is defined by four *quantum numbers* for which the usual symbols are n, l, m_l, and m_s. These numbers can take only discrete values; the first three can be only whole numbers, the last, m_s, may be only $+\frac{1}{2}$ or $-\frac{1}{2}$. (Zero is counted as a whole number.) The permissible values of the first three quantum numbers are interrelated. The value of n places certain restrictions on the permissible values of l, the value of l places restrictions on the permissible values of m_l.

(2) Two quantum states are different if *any* of the four quantum numbers describing the two states is different. The question of when two quantum states are different is important because within a single system (such as a single atom, for example) all the electrons

16

must be in different quantum states. This last statement is known as the Pauli Exclusion Principle, and is roughly (very, very roughly) equivalent to saying that two things cannot occupy the same place at the same time.

(3) In principle, all four quantum numbers may be required to calculate the energy of an electron in a particular quantum state. In the isolated atom, however, only the values of n and l are important. The permissible values of n and l generate a series of permissible energy levels in which the electrons are to be found. These levels are named according to the value of the first two quantum numbers, with a number that is actually the value of n, and (for purely historical reasons) a letter designating the value of l for that level, according to the following scheme:

Scheme for naming energy shells by the value of the first two quantum numbers, n and l. The number is the value of n, and the letter identifies the value of l; that is, in any s-shell, $l = 0$, in any p-shell, $l = 1$, and so on. Quantum states where l is larger than $n - 1$ do not exist

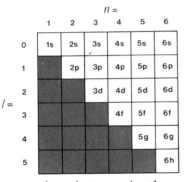

Thus the $4f$ level, for example, contains electrons in those quantum states in which $n = 4$ and $l = 3$. As the reader may observe from the blanks in the table, the value of l for any quantum state may not exceed $n - 1$. Thus there is no $1p$ level (which would correspond to $n = 1 : l = 1$, but this is not a possible, or permissible, quantum state).

(4) The value of l for a given energy level fixes the number of *different* quantum states available at that level, and thus, by Pauli's principle, the maximum number of electrons that can occupy that level. This number is $4l + 2$. Thus any s-shell ($l = 0$) can contain a maximum of $4(0) + 2 = 2$ electrons, any p-shell ($l = 1$) a maximum of $4(1) + 2 = 6$ electrons, any d-shell ($l = 2$) a maximum of 10 electrons, etc.

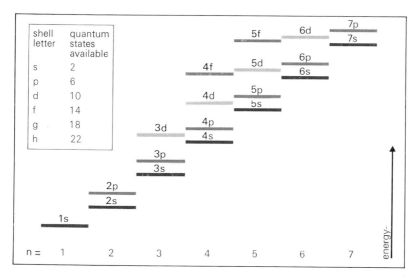

shell letter	quantum states available
s	2
p	6
d	10
f	14
g	18
h	22

Relative electron energies for electrons in different quantum states in an isolated atom.

The relative energy levels with the number of electrons that can be accommodated in each, given in the legend, are shown on the accompanying diagram. Note that the energy level depends primarily on the value of n, the first quantum number, but that there is some overlap, due to the various values of l. Thus an electron in the 4s-subshell has less energy than one in the 3d-subshell, and that the amount of overlap increases with higher values of n. Note also that the largest energy " jumps " on the diagram occur between p-shells and the next s-shells, except for the jump between the 1s- and 2s-shells, where there is no intervening p-shell.

A physical system is most stable in the state where its total energy is the least; therefore the electrons in each kind of atom tend to occupy the lowest-energy states at first. The one electron of a hydrogen atom is most likely to be found in a 1s quantum state; in helium (He, Z = 2) both electrons can occupy 1s states (since there are two different quantum states at the 1s level). In lithium (Li, Z = 3) the third electron is forced into a 2s state, however, since only two 1s quantum states are possible in a single system. Similar considerations apply to more complex atoms.

The arrangement of electrons into energy shells, for selected elements, is shown in the diagram on the facing page. Note that, in keeping with the relative energy level diagram (page 17), the 4s-shell in potassium (K, Z = 19) and calcium (Ca, Z = 20) is filled before the 3d-shell fills. Note also that as a p-shell fills, the elements pass from metal, through metalloids to " typical non-metals," and finally to noble gases, when the p-shell contains its maximum number of electrons, 6. This is particularly well seen in the series from beryllium (Be, Z = 4) to neon (Ne, Z = 10).

The relative energy diagram on page 17 serves to compare energy levels within the same atom only. The actual energy levels depend on the atomic number Z, as well as on n and l. The greater the positive charge on the nucleus (which is, of course, + Z—that is, +1 for H, +2 for He, +3 for Li, etc.) the more tightly are all the electrons bound to the nucleus, and the lower are all energy levels in that atom. The actual energies of the most energetic (that is, outermost) electrons for selected elements are shown in the right-hand part of the diagram on the right. (The " zero " of this scale is the energy that would just allow the electron to escape the atom altogether; hence all the values shown are negative.) The highest occupied level in both hydrogen and helium is the 1s level. Note how the increase of Z from 1 (hydrogen) to 2 (helium) decreases the energy of the electrons at this 1s level.

The diagram shows how the energy of the highest occupied state " jumps " when an electron must be put in a previously unoccupied s level. These jumps, noted on the diagram by the double-headed arrows, are the same jumps seen on the relative energy diagram, with the effect of Z now taken into account. The highest electron energies are seen in the alkali metals, lithium (Li), sodium (Na), potassium (K), and cesium (Cs). The more familiar metals, iron (Fe), cobalt (Co), and nickel (Ni), are not far behind, and the values given for these metals are fairly typical. The lowest energies for outer shells are found in the noble gases with the typically non-metallic halogens, fluorine (Fl), chlorine (Cl), and bromine (Br), with little greater energies. The important difference between the unreactive noble gases and the fiercely active halogens is that the outer shell in the noble gases is full, while the halogens have an unoccupied quantum state at a low energy level.

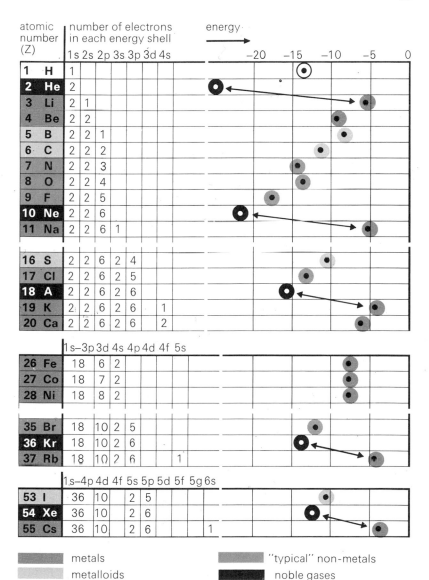

metals

"typical" non-metals

metalloids

noble gases

(hydrogen not classified)

Electron arrangement and energies for outermost electrons for selected elements (see text).

The Ionic Bond

Typical nonmetals are elements in which the p-shell is only one or two electrons short of being completely filled. The available quantum states in such a typical nonmetal are thus of low energy. Such an empty state will be energetically attractive to a high-energy electron from another element, usually a metal. For example, chlorine (Cl, $Z = 17$) has only 5 electrons in its outer or $3p$-shell, and the atomic number of chlorine (17) is so much higher than that of sodium (11) that the $3p$ energy level of chlorine is lower than the $3s$ level of sodium. (Notice the actual energy levels for the outermost electrons of sodium (Na) and chlorine (Cl) in the diagram on page 19.) Thus the electron from the $3s$ level of sodium may move to the unoccupied lower-energy quantum state in the $3p$ level of the chlorine atom and release energy in the process. In general, the outermost electrons of metals occupy relatively energetic quantum states. The metals thus tend to lose electrons and form positive ions; the nonmetals tend to form negative ions.

In the formation of sodium chloride, when the electron from the sodium deserts, it leaves the sodium atom with a net positive electrical charge of $+1$, as we saw before, and conversely, the

Formation of sodium chloride (NaCl). The single electron from the $3s$-shell of sodium loses energy by moving to the unoccupied quantum state in the $3p$ level of chlorine. (See diagram on page 19 for the actual energies involved.)

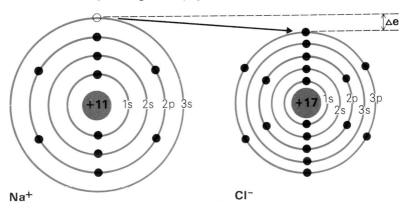

Na⁺   Cl⁻

chlorine atom acquires a charge of -1, so that the two atoms become Na^+ and Cl^- ions, respectively. The resulting electrostatic attraction between the negatively and positively charged ions binds these two kinds of ions into the crystal structure we illustrated earlier (page 13). We should not allow the mechanics of this bond to obscure the more fundamental condition that allows the bond to exist—that the system as a whole has less energy in the bonded state than the same number of atoms would have as isolated atoms. The decrease in energy in this case comes from the drop in energy of the electron that has moved from the $3s$ level of the sodium atom to the $3p$ level of the chlorine atom. The fundamental condition for any kind of bond to form is that the bonded state should represent a decrease in energy over the unbonded state.

The integrity of an ionic crystal depends on the alternate arrangement of positive and negative ions, and it is not hard to see why such a structure will be brittle and intolerant of irregularities. A minor irregularity in the arrangement will have serious results. For example, in an NaCl crystal, if one Na^+ ion were missing from its place in the lattice, its six neighbors (all Cl^- ions) would actively repel each other. If one plane of the crystal were to slide over another by one crystal spacing, bringing Cl^- ions next to Cl^- ions, and Na^+ ions next to Na^+ ions, the planes would actively fly apart. Thus, while perfect ionic crystals are in principle quite strong, actual ionic crystals, containing the inevitable irregularities, are usually easily crumbled.

The Covalent Bond

Ionic bonds can be formed only between atoms of different elements—that is, there must be one kind of atom that gives up electrons to form positive ions and a second kind that accepts electrons to form the negative ions. The metal crystal, with which we are primarily concerned, need not contain more than one kind of atom—a copper crystal may be pure copper, for example—and thus the bond between metal atoms cannot be ionic. We must find other mechanisms for bonding between atoms of the same element. The covalent or " shared-electron-pair " bond will serve as a good introduction to this subject, although it differs from the metallic bond in many important respects.

In the table on page 16 we made a preliminary classification of the quantum states electrons might occupy in the isolated atom by considering the first two quantum numbers, n and l only. Thus the $3d$ group of quantum states contains those states where $n = 3$ and $l = 2$, and so forth. Our justification for considering only the first two quantum numbers, and ignoring the values of the other two quantum numbers, m_l and m_s, was that in an isolated atom the electrons in quantum states within a given group all had essentially the same energy. Indeed, we refer to the $1s$ energy level, or the $3d$ energy level, and so on. We must recall, however, that each of these groups does contain several different quantum states; that is, any s group consists of 2 different quantum states, any p group of 6 different quantum states, and so on. When atoms are brought sufficiently close together that their electron shells can interact, the quantum states are modified, and the resulting quantum states may no longer have the same energy, even within the same group. Under appropriate circumstances this may lead to bonding between atoms of the same element.

A simple case occurs in hydrogen gas. At ordinary temperatures hydrogen gas is found as molecules consisting of two hydrogen atoms each, rather than as single atoms. The hydrogen atom has only a single electron, and this electron is normally in the lowest energy state available, a $1s$ state. If two hydrogen atoms approach each other, however, the $1s$ energy level splits into two branches, one of greater energy than the $1s$ level of the isolated hydrogen atom and one of lesser energy. By our general rule that nature tends to run downhill, the two electrons (one from each atom) tend to occupy the lower energy branch of the split $1s$ level, and so the two-atom hydrogen molecule is formed. The energy lost by the two electrons in the process is given off, usually as heat. In order to separate the two atoms again work would have to be done (to raise the electrons to their original energy level) and so the two-atom molecule of hydrogen is the stable state.

The bond just described is called a *covalent*, or *shared-electron-pair*, bond. The two electrons, one from each hydrogen atom, are thought to resonate about a position intermediate between the two hydrogen nuclei, and it is no longer possible to say that one electron belongs to one hydrogen nucleus and the other electron to the other nucleus. All we can say is that one pair of electrons is shared between the two nuclei. In the metallic bond, to be discussed shortly, we shall see another kind of electron-sharing, on a much larger scale. The term *covalent*, however, is applied only to shared-electron-pair bonds, as these bonds have certain characteristics that set them apart from systems in which many electrons are shared between many nuclei.

Covalent bonds can be formed between atoms more complex than hydrogen atoms, and also between atoms of different elements. Further, a single atom may form more than one covalent bond. Thus in the diamond crystal, which is pure carbon, each carbon atom forms four covalent bonds with four neighboring carbon atoms. In each of these four bonds it shares a specific pair of electrons with a specific neighboring atom. Such bonds may be quite strong, as the diamond example shows. In covalent bonds, however, distance is critical and when a single atom forms more than one covalent bond, the angle between bonds is quite critical also. The result is that the diamond crystal, although the hardest substance known, is also very brittle.

The Metallic Bond

The metallic bond, for which the reader has waited so patiently, is neither covalent nor ionic. It has some features of each, but differs importantly from both. In a metal crystal we find a regular structure of metal atoms from which the outer one or two electrons are " missing," leaving the atoms in the form of positively charged ions. In many cases these ions are packed together as closely as the geometry of the situation permits. But where are the " missing " electrons, and why does this structure not simply fly apart, due to the mutual repulsion of the similarly charged ions?

The " missing " electrons are still in the crystal; indeed, in a sense we shall note directly, they are " closer " to the rest of the atom (the positive ion) than they were in the isolated atom. All the electrons, those still in the ions and the " missing " electrons as well, are still governed by strict quantum considerations, just as in the isolated atom. However, the presence of many nuclei in the metal crystal modifies the quantum levels available to the electrons in a very important way. The electrons remaining with the ion are

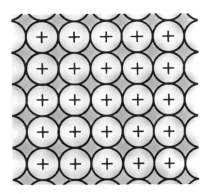

Schematic representation of a metal crystal. The positive ions are arranged in a regular (here rectangular) pattern. The balancing negative charges (suggested by the blue patches) are not localized but range throughout the crystal.

the least affected, and those in the inner shells hardly know that there are any other atoms about. For the outer or valence electrons, however, the lowest energy states now available describe " orbits " extending throughout the entire crystal, so that it is no longer possible to say that any particular electron pertains to any particular nucleus or ion. Insofar as it is permissible to speak of the location of an electron, we can say that there are always sufficient electrons in the vicinity of a given positive ion to maintain the electrical neutrality of the system, but not in any simple or continuing way.

We shall see in Chapter 2 that not all the bonding in a metallic crystal is due to the circulating electrons. There is some interaction between the outer electrons of the metallic ions as well, and it is possible to think of direct ion-to-ion bonds. The amount of energy involved in these secondary bonds is small, however, compared to that involved in the circulating electrons. The secondary, or ion-to-ion, bonds may influence the form of the crystal, but the real " glue " that holds the crystal together is the attraction between the circulating electrons and the positive ions.

In the simplest sense, then, we may think of the basic mechanism responsible for the metal crystal as this attraction between the ions and the circulating electrons. But this is clearly only the beginning of the story, since why should these circulating electrons not be captured by the individual ions? The reason, as we stated above, is that, in the crystal structure, there are no available quantum states for those electrons, which permit them to be associated with

Energy bands in an isolated sodium atom (left) and in a sodium crystal (right). Since the 3s band in the atom contains only one electron, but provides two quantum states, half of the quantum states (normally the higher energy half) of the split 3s band are unoccupied. The inner levels are unaffected at normal crystal spacings.

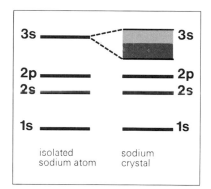

particular ions. The circulating electrons in the crystal are not captured by individual ions for the same reason that electrons in an isolated atom do not simply fall into the nucleus. Electrons can exist only in permissible quantum states, and the states that would permit either kind of collapse do not exist.

Now, what of the energy of these circulating electrons? The diagram on this page compares the energy levels in a sodium crystal with the energy levels in an isolated sodium atom. The inner levels (1s, 2s, and 2p) are virtually unaffected; but the outer level (3s) has split into a whole band of energy levels. In an isolated sodium atom, there is only one electron at the 3s level, but that level (or any s level) provides two different quantum states, one of which is unoccupied in the isolated sodium atom. In a sodium crystal consisting of, say, one million million sodium atoms, this 3s band provides *two* million million different quantum states. There are only one million million circulating electrons, one from each sodium atom, so half the quantum states in the band are unoccupied. By our general rule that nature tends to run downhill, the circulating electrons in the crystal occupy the quantum states in the lower half of the energy band. Their average energy is less than the energy they would have in the isolated atom; therefore the crystal is stable. Work would have to be done—energy supplied—to disassemble the crystal; the energy required is the energy needed to raise the circulating electrons from their lower energy states in the crystal to the higher energy states they must occupy in the isolated atom. The metallic bond, then, meets the same general condition as our two previous types of bonds, that is, the energy of the system in the bonded state is less than the energy of the same number of isolated atoms.

So far all we have shown is that the metal crystal will not spontaneously dissolve into a dust of constituent atoms. The reader may have been prepared to grant this point without all the argument. Our original purpose, however, was to account for the tolerance of the metal crystal for imperfections in structure—that is, for the ductility of metals—and we are now finally in a position to discuss this question, i.e. the reason why metals bend, although diamonds, glass, and salt crystals break.

An interatomic bond is broken if, for any reason, the binding electrons are forced into states of higher energy than those they would occupy in an isolated atom. When this happens the unbonded state is the stable, or lower-energy, state. An irregularity in crystal structure may cause such an energy rise by altering interatomic spacings or by distorting bond angles. In ionic or covalent crystals, the bonding force is a local affair, and an irregularity will cause a sharp local energy rise. The increase in total energy of the entire crystal may be trivially small, but this is no consolation to the electrons directly involved. Their energy is increased above that of the unbonded state and so the bond is broken.

The situation is quite different in the metal crystal. The electrons responsible for the basic binding force range over the entire crystal, and a single irregularity may, and in principle does, affect the energy level of every electron in the crystal. Since the effect of the irregularity is spread over all, or at least a very large number of, electrons, however, no single electron is affected very much. The total energy rise may be as great as in an ionic or covalent crystal, but since many electrons share this energy rise, none is placed in an energetically untenable position.

Our argument here is oversimplified and somewhat overdrawn. We shall see in Chapter 2 that an irregularity does cause some local energy rise in a metal crystal, due to distortion of the secondary or ion-to-ion bonds. But in the metal crystal these secondary bonds exist within the comfortable context of the primary binding force furnished by the circulating electrons, and when broken will have a

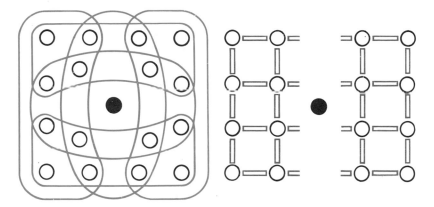

Effects of irregularity in metallic (left) and nonmetallic (right) crystals. The effect of the irregularity in the metal crystal is spread over all the bonds in the crystal ; in the nonmetallic crystal, the effect is localized, breaking the bonds in the immediate neighborhood.

chance to reform. In the ionic or covalent crystal, the ion-to-ion or atom-to-atom bonds, though much stronger, stand alone, and if broken, there is no immediate reason why they should be restored.

The oversimplification in our argument is this: We said an irregularity forced all, or at least a great many, of the circulating electrons into quantum states of very slightly higher energy than they would otherwise occupy. We have stressed that quantum considerations are absolute; electrons can acquire additional energy only if the appropriate quantum states exist in the system and are available, i.e. unoccupied. We can only argue here that the existence of the appropriate quantum states is made plausible by the fact that our circulating electrons in the perfect crystal occupy quantum states in the lower part of a continuous energy band in which unoccupied states of higher energy exist (diagram, page 25). The situation is quite different in the isolated atom, where a given electron could change energy only by discrete " quantum jumps " from one fixed energy level to another. In the metal crystal, appropriate quantum states exist for any small energy change, as long as this does not carry the electron out of the band.

Bands of permissible energy levels are found in ionic and covalent crystals as well as in metal crystals, but in these nonmetallic crystals the bands are full—all quantum states occupied. The electrons have no more flexibility than if they were restricted to a single energy level, because an electron desiring to change energy has no unoccupied quantum state within the band into which it can move. In the metal crystal, the electrons in the partially unoccupied energy band—and these are the electrons responsible for the primary binding in the metal crystal—are free, in terms of .available quantum states, to change energy by arbitrarily small amounts. Some authorities cite this freedom, with the condition that gives rise to it, as the essential and defining characteristic of the metallic state.

We have not completed our argument leading to the ductility of metals. What we have shown is that local irregularities do not have as serious a result for a metal crystal as they do for a nonmetallic crystal. Given the overall cohesive force furnished by the circulating electrons, local irregularities in a metal crystal tend to be self-healing; in the nonmetallic crystals, where overall cohesive force is lacking, the irregularities are not self-healing. We shall resume this argument, showing the effect of these local irregularities, in Chapter 2, but before doing so we want to relate some other characteristics of metals to what has been said so far.

The range of energies represented by available quantum states in metals as opposed to other solids is strikingly shown by the electrical conductivity of metals. For a solid to conduct electricity, electrons must move within the solid. This involves change in energy for the electrons, and will require them to move from their previous quantum states to new states of higher energy. In metals we find that the amount of current that flows is strictly proportional to the applied voltage. In particular, there is no minimum voltage below which no current will flow. There are always available quantum states into which the electrons can move, no matter how small the amount of energy we add.

In a typical nonmetallic solid, such as glass or ceramic material or a (dry) salt crystal, no appreciable current flows even with quite large applied voltages. With sufficiently high voltages a *breakdown voltage* is finally reached at which current begins to flow. This breakdown voltage represents the energy necessary to move the electrons from the filled energy bands, within which they cannot be accelerated, across an energy gap in which no permissible quantum states exist, to a higher energy band of previously unoccupied quantum states. The semiconductors, now so important in transistor technology, are materials in which this " energy gap " between the filled bands and the nearest available band of unfilled quantum states is very small, compared to the gap existing in the nonconductors. In metals, as we have said, this gap does not exist.

Another property usually cited as characteristic of metals is luster. Metals are shiny; they reflect light rather than absorbing it or transmitting it. We cannot take the space here to recite the whole argument. It turns out, however, that this characteristic luster also derives from the freedom of the circulating electrons in the metal to move between quantum states of closely related energy.

In this chapter we have suggested the reasons for the tolerance of metal crystals for local irregularities. In Chapter 2 we shall see how these irregularities control the properties of the metal and are themselves controlled.

2 Crystals, Dislocations, and Alloys

The three chief forms taken by metal crystals, the hexagonal close-packed (HCP), the face-centered cubic (FCC), and the body-centered cubic (BCC) are illustrated in detail on the two following pages. The fact that different metals take different crystalline forms (and the same metal may take different forms under different conditions) is evidence of the " secondary bonding " in the metal crystal to which we referred in Chapter 1. The metal ions making up the crystal are not hard, featureless spheres with definite boundaries. The outer electron shells of the ions may overlap and interact, and energy is involved in these interactions. Within the overall binding force furnished by the circulating electrons within the crystal, the ions assume those relative spacings and positions that minimize the overall energy of the crystal, taking the energy involved in the ion-to-ion interactions into account, of course.

Two of the common crystalline forms, the hexagonal close packed and the face-centered cubic, are in principle " close-packed "—that is, both of them crowd as many spheres into a

Experiments with " bubble rafts " (spontaneously formed configurations of bubbles of uniform size on a liquid surface or, as here, on wet glass) suggest the process of grain formation in metals. Perfectly regular areas, analogous to perfect crystals, as well as " dislocations " and " grain boundaries," can be seen.

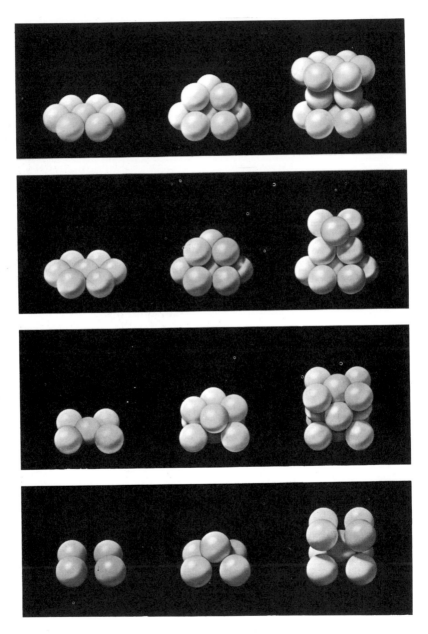

Both the hexagonal close-packed (HCP) crystal and the face-centered cubic (FCC) crystal are built up of identical hexagonal close-packed planes. In the HCP crystals (left) the third layer is placed directly over the first layer, giving an ABABAB arrangement. In the FCC crystal (below left) the third layer is not directly over either of the first two layers, giving an ABCABCABC arrangement as shown.

Left: The FCC crystal, showing placement of the third layer. Right: The same crystal with a fourth layer added directly over the first layer, and with additional ions (shaded) to show a face of the " face-centered cube " from which the crystal is named.

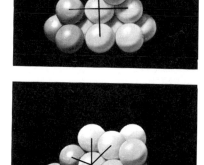

Left: The same FCC crystal built up from rectangular planes. Right: The FCC crystal dissected to show a hexagonal plane formed by stacking rectangular planes. In both the HCP and FCC crystals each ion has twelve close neighbors.

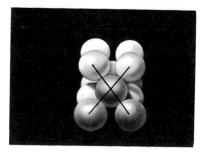

Left: The body-centered cubic (BCC) crystal. This consists of two identical simple rectangular lattices with the " corners " of one lattice occupying the center of the " cubes " formed by the other lattice. It contains no close-packed planes. Each ion has 6 close neighbors, four of which are seen in the view at right.

given volume as is geometrically possible. As the illustrations show, both are composed of close-packed hexagonal planes, one stacked on another. In the HCP form, however, it is commonly found that, in fact, the spacing between planes is somewhat greater than would be required if the ions were spherical. The ions behave as if they were ovoid, with their long axes perpendicular to the hexagonal plane. The third major form, the body-centered cubic, contains no close-packed planes, and therefore (to the extent that the ions are spherical) contains some waste space. One must be very cautious about drawing conclusions about the mechanical properties of a metal from its characteristic crystal habit, however. In what follows we shall show the crystal lattice as a simple rectangular pattern, and the reader must imagine that what is said of this simple pattern applies, with suitable modifications, to the more complex patterns in real metals.

Sources of Dislocations

To deform a perfect metal crystal, whole planes of ions would have to slide over each other, one plane at a time. As we said in Chapter 1, this would require enormous forces, far beyond those required to deform actual metals. The reason why these large forces are not required is that irregularities in crystal structure allow the crystal to deform under much less stress, as we shall see shortly. Since these irregularities (or dislocations, as they are called by the metallurgist) are so important in understanding metals, it is desirable to see why they occur.

How a screw dislocation permits crystal growth. Individual ions can "stick" in the step formed by the dislocation more easily than on the plane surface of a perfect crystal.

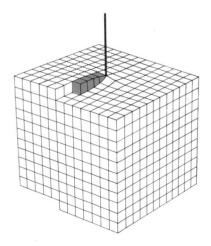

There are three major reasons for dislocations. The first is fundamental and inescapable. A perfect crystal would be the most stable form only at the absolute zero of temperature, −273°C. At normal temperature, crystals containing a certain number of dislocations, particularly vacancies where an ion is missing from its place in the lattice, are actually the more stable form. The second reason is perhaps more important. A perfect crystal, by virtue of its perfection and completeness, is likely to grow less rapidly (as a metal cools from the molten state, for example) than a crystal containing a notch or imperfection where a wandering ion from the molten metal can lodge. At least one common irregularity, called a *screw* dislocation, is apparently caused by such a process of crystal growth. Finally, dislocations arise by pure historical accident, by mechanical deformation of the lattice, and as a result of chemical attack on the surface of the metal.

The two simplest kinds of dislocations are the *vacancy* and the *interstitial*. In the first, an ion is simply missing from its place in the lattice; in the second, an extra ion has become lodged between two rows. In practice these kinds of dislocations are actually more likely to involve whole rows or planes of atoms, which end abruptly in the interior of the crystal. The screw dislocation is of this type.

Effect of Dislocations

Whatever the source of the dislocation, it brings about a strain on the crystal lattice, causing a local concentration of energy. Such a high-energy region is less stable than the unstrained portion of

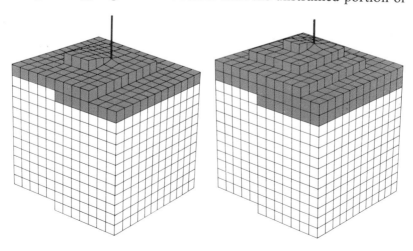

the lattice, and can be altered with lower applied stress. The effect is shown in the diagram below. Under relatively light stress, the dislocation moves across the crystal, like the ruck across a carpet, a single line at a step, until at the end the top rows are displaced a whole lattice step with respect to the bottom rows. The effect is the same as if the whole row had slipped at once, but since the slippage took place at a single line at a time, much smaller forces are involved. Further, the crystal is stronger after the displacement has occurred than it was before, because the dislocation has disappeared in the process. In practice, other dislocations would probably arise simultaneously, so the crystal is no stronger after the dislocation has moved; the important point is that it is not weaker. This ability to deform, and to retain the deformation after the deforming stress is removed, without any substantial weakening of the material, is what is meant by the characteristic ductility of metals.

The reader may well be puzzled here, because we think of metals as strong, while what we have just shown is that they are weak, and deform under relatively light stresses. In fact, pure metals containing a moderate number of dislocations free to move about, are generally too soft or weak to be of much mechanical use. Pure aluminum or copper rods the size of a thick pencil are, in fact, easily bent with the bare hands, and pure iron rods are not much stronger. The conventional ways of making metals strong enough for practical use are all based, ultimately, on hampering the movement of the dislocations that give metal its ductility.

How a dislocation permits crystal deformation. At the far right, the top row is displaced one whole crystal with respect to the bottom row, but only one line of ions must move at any one time.

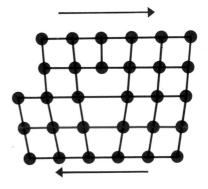

Again the reader may be puzzled. We said that the ductility, and ultimately the practical strength, of the metal derives from the movement of dislocations within the metal crystals. If we hamper this movement, or stop it altogether, are we not in the same position as if we had used a nonmetal in which the dislocations are naturally immobile at the outset? The answer, in part at least, is that in metals we can control the degree of mobility of the dislocations, to get the balance between ductility and breaking strength (with its accompanying brittleness) required by the application. Further, if we are artful enough about it, we can sometimes get, not the best, but almost the best, of both characteristics. With this in mind, let us see what hampers the movement of dislocations.

A dislocation can move easily across a crystal lattice only because the lattice is a regular structure. If it were completely disordered, the kind of systematic movement illustrated previously for a dislocation would be quite impossible. The most obvious barrier to dislocation movement in these terms, then, is another dislocation. Metals containing moderate amounts of dislocations are ductile; if there are too many dislocations, however, they will interfere with each other's movement, and the metal will become brittle. Very little useful strengthening of metal can be brought about by introducing more dislocations, but this effect is suspected of being very important in the development of metal fatigue, as we shall see directly.

The grain boundaries are another obvious barrier to dislocation movement. Practical metals are composed of numerous single

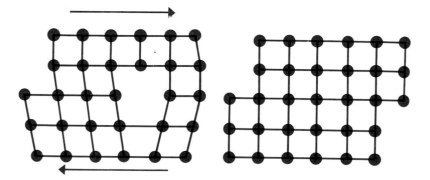

crystals, or grains, and at the border between two grains the lattice is completely disordered, for the distance of a few atomic diameters, at least. Such borders are effective barriers to dislocation movement, and in general, the larger the grain size in a metal the greater the ductility. Most metals " work-harden "—that is, if they are hammered or repeatedly bent, they lose ductility and become brittle. Much of this effect is due to breaking up the grains into smaller grains. Again very little useful strengthening of metals is achieved this way, but the effect is important in metalworking, and explains why it is sometimes necessary to reheat metal after mechanical working, to allow the broken-up grains to reform into larger grains again.

The most useful, and most easily controlled, method of " freezing " the dislocations is *alloying*—that is, the mixture of several different metals, or sometimes nonmetals, with the basic metal. We shall discuss alloying in more detail later. The major effect of alloying additions, however, is to distort the crystal lattice, thereby making it difficult for the dislocations to move. However, other effects are involved as well, as we shall see.

Deformation and Fracture

In discussing the mechanical deformation of metals, we think of applying a force, usually measured in tons, to stretch a bar of standard cross-section. Thus if we apply a force of 10 tons to a bar whose cross-section is one quarter inch square the applied *stress* is 40 tons per square inch. The resulting elongation of the bar is called the *strain*, and may be measured as a percentage of the original length. In metals, the initial strain is elastic, as in brittle nonmetals. If the deforming stress is removed, the metal returns to its original length. Furthermore, during elastic strain, the strain is proportional to the stress; that is, if a stress of five tons per square inch will lengthen the bar by one tenth of one per cent (·1 per cent strain), twice that stress will cause a strain of ·2 per cent. Therefore, on a stress-strain diagram, the region of elastic strain shows as a sharply-rising straight line. In terms of what we have said about crystals, we can think of this initial elastic strain as due to stretching of interatomic bonds, with little permanent movement of dislocations.

Few practical metals show elastic strains as great as one half of one per cent (·5 per cent). If the stress is increased beyond the point causing such strain (the plastic yield point of the metal), deformation sets in as the mobile dislocations now move to allow whole planes of atoms to slide over one another. When the stress is removed, the plastic portion of the strain remains. During initial plastic deformation, the metal does not fail; it may actually become stronger, due to the " work-hardening " described earlier. Finally, if the stress is increased sufficiently, the metal will part in a ductile fracture. The ultimate breaking strength for steels, for example, may occur at stresses half again as high as that reached at the plastic yield point. For very ductile metals, with low plastic yield points, the ultimate breaking stress may be several times greater than the stress at the plastic yield point.

For the applications engineer, the maximum useful strength of the metal is the plastic yield point, since permanent changes in dimensions of metal parts can hardly be tolerated; and, of course, he works below this point to have some safety margins. Now, we have said that only a few dislocations in the metal move before the

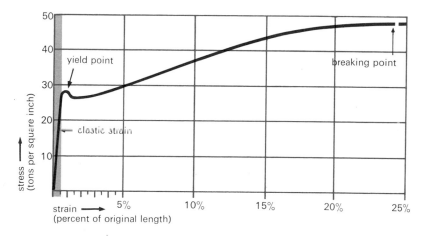

Stress-strain diagram for mild steel. The initial elastic strain, in the shaded region of the diagram, is reversible if the stress is removed. The strengthening of the steel after the initial yield point has been reached is due to " work-hardening."

plastic yield point is reached; why, then, should this point occur at greater stress in metals than in brittle nonmetals, where the dislocations are permanently immobile? The reason is that the movement of some dislocations in metals below the plastic yield point prevents local concentrations of stress that would allow cracks to spread and the specimen to part.

To appreciate this point it is necessary to realize the enormous local stresses that can develop at the tip of a crack in a brittle solid even where the overall stress is relatively low. The sides of the crack focus the force on the few unfortunate bonds at the tip of the crack, so that the effective stress on those bonds exceeds the theoretical strength of the crystal; they are broken, and the crack, attacking a few bonds at a time, spreads rapidly over the material, resulting in complete brittle fracture. This is what happens when a diamond crystal is struck with a sharply pointed tool, for example. In the metal, mobile dislocations move to the tip of the crack, blunting it and spreading the force over a larger region, thereby reducing the effective stress. The brittle solid never gets a chance to show its theoretical strength because cracks allow local stress concentrations to exceed that theoretical strength even when the overall stress is much less. In metals the movement of dislocations to the tip of such a crack, or other such local area of high stress, distributes the load to a larger number of bonds, and stops the crack. The limit of the useful strength of the metal is thus set by the stress at which these dislocations allow plastic deformation to begin.

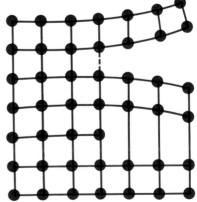

Effect of a dislocation in stopping a crack. When the dislocation has moved to the base of the crack, the force is spread over a larger area, and the effective stress is lowered.

We have been discussing the practical strength of materials in terms of how cracks spread in the material. The reason is that in almost all practical materials, there are inevitable surface defects from which cracks may develop and spread, and the more brittle the material, the more it is weakened by such surface defects. Experiments made on glass show the relationship between surface defects, cracks, ultimate strength, and ductility very nicely. For practical purposes the ductility of glass at room temperature is zero. A piece of well-made precision glass, carefully treated to eliminate surface defects, will support a stress as high as 400 tons per square inch, which is a great deal more than our best steels will support. Such a stress must be applied very carefully, of course, so that there is no tendency to twist or bend the glass. When the glass is under such a stress, however, merely touching it with a sharp diamond crystal will cause it to shatter explosively. Pure aluminum, by contrast, will barely support a stress of three tons per square inch before plastic deformation begins. Surface scratches on such a piece of aluminum have virtually no effect, however.

The standard way of assessing the brittleness of metal is to cut a notch of standard size and shape in a standard bar and to hit the bar a sharp but measured blow. The more brittle the material, the lighter the blow required to break it at the site of the notch. The shape of the notch is important as well, a sharp pointed notch producing a greater weakness than one with a blunt tip. The more ductile the material, the less " notch-sensitive " it is. Alloying

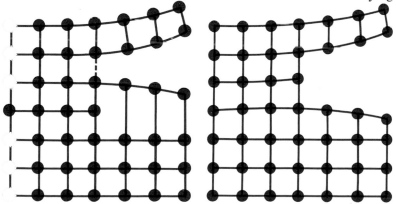

techniques that freeze up a large portion of the dislocations in a metal raise the elastic yield point of the metal, but, unless one resorts to some of the sophisticated tricks described in Chapter 5, will increase the notch sensitivity as well. For example, steels that will support static loads of over 200 tons per square inch have been developed, but these steels are so brittle that they are useless for most applications. The task of the metallurgist is to design, or choose between, various alloys that give the best balance of strength and sensitivity.

So far we have discussed the deformation and fracture of metals as they occur in a single test or stress cycle. But such single tests do not tell the whole story, by any means. Under repeated stress cycling, or under a stress maintained for long periods, metals may fail by fatigue or by creep. Both are mechanisms that lead to failure by the metal in service at stresses that may be much below the plastic yield point of the metal.

Fatigue and Creep

Metal fatigue has been made famous by the aircraft industry because there its effects have been the most dramatic, but it is no less common in other environments. Whenever a component is subjected to a large number of stress oscillations (to vibrations) there is a danger that eventually it will become fatigued and snap with little or no advance warning. Creep is a less spectacular effect, which, because it is more predictable, rarely goes as far as an actual failure. It is no less important, though, for, consisting as it does of gradual plastic deformation of the metal, it involves dimensional changes that, although perhaps only a few thousandths of an inch, can be critical in precision equipment such as gas- or steam-turbines, with their necessarily small blade clearances.

Most failures of metals in service are caused by fatigue. The back-axle that snaps as you set off on holiday is fatigued, just as is the aircraft wing, the spring, or the rivet. In all cases the failure usually occurs after the stress has oscillated a few thousands of times, even though the overall maximum stress is relatively low. Other factors can intervene to aggravate fatigue, such as corrosion, or design that produces unnecessary stress concentrations, but the main feature is the repeated cycling of the stress.

Theories on how fatigue failure comes about are numerous and complex, involving minute studies of crystalline structures. Here we can only give an outline of some of the things that seem to be important, and see how they fit our necessarily simplified view of the metallic crystal.

The first thing that we notice about a fatigue failure is that the metal undergoes scarcely any plastic deformation before it breaks, and this only at the last moment. Thus there is no easy way of seeing that the metal is liable to fracture. Only a close microscopic examination could reveal the fine cracks that were leading to disaster, and then only if they were at the surface, which, although commonly so, is not always the case. A look at a fatigue fracture usually shows that the failure has taken place in three stages. In the first stage the crack is smooth and there are wave-markings rather like those on a beach, propagating, in most cases, from a single source at the surface of the metal. During this stage the crack has grown slowly, pausing frequently.

As the area carrying the load grows smaller with the spread of the fatigue crack, the stress on the remaining metal rises, and eventually the second phase of fracture sets in, with the crack propagating much more quickly, leaving a rougher zone, but still without any signs of plastic deformation. In the third fracture stage the load-carrying area is now so small that the elastic limit is exceeded and the metal deforms plastically and separates.

What is most clear from this is that somehow the metal has not been protected from crack propagation by the mechanism as described earlier; it has apparently fractured just like a brittle nonmetal, even though normal tensile tests may have shown the metal to be quite ductile. How has this come about?

All fatigue cracks develop from some point in the metal around which stresses have become concentrated, although not so intensely that they are relieved by massive plastic flow. This point may be a fault at the surface—a scratch or tool mark, or an accumulation of vacancies—or it could be due to the particular design of the component that, whether unavoidable or not, allows stress to concentrate around a joint, a channel, or similar surface features. Under static loading conditions such concentrations would have little effect until the overall stress approached the elastic limit of the metal, when they would begin to strain plastically as more and more dislocations moved into their area. As the stress increased further, these dislocations would begin to interfere with one another, and eventually a state would be reached where no more could move into the area. The point of stress would now be brittle, and cracks could begin to develop, leading rapidly to failure. In the case where the stress is relatively low and rapidly alternating—the usual conditions of fatigue—the same sort of buildup takes place, but with important differences. At each cycle only a small number of dislocations is likely to move into an area of stress concentration, and there is no chance for plastic flow, which involves whole planes of atoms slipping over one another, helped by large numbers of dislocations. As the stress cycling continues, so does the gradual infiltration of dislocations into areas of concentration. Eventually, as with the increasing uncycled load, interference develops until a point is reached at which no more dislocations can move in; the metal is brittle and a crack spreads across the small hardened area around the originating fault. But this is as far as it goes, for now the crack reaches a ductile region, and the whole process begins again. In the case of a high static load this new buildup would be quite rapid, so that the metal could tear fairly continuously. In the first stage of fatigue-crack propagation it is slow, and the crack spreads intermittently, giving the waveformation of the diagram on pages 40-41. By the time the second stage is reached (though sometimes this stage is bypassed) the buildup is rapid enough for the crack to spread almost continuously, although still in a brittle manner. And finally, the stress concentration is so high that a single cycle is enough to finish the job off with a rapid ductile fracture.

Exactly how fatigue cracks start, how dislocations interact to give eventual hardening, why the fracture is almost wholly brittle, what effect environment and details of design have, why some stress concentrations cause fatigue while others do not, and how to detect potential for fatigue failure early in the life of a component—all these are problems faced by the metallurgist and designer thinking about metal fatigue. The explanation we have given here is only a simple starting point; but there is still no really comprehensive theory of fatigue that answers all the questions.

Comprehensive testing in the laboratory is still the only really useful weapon the metallurgist has to help him decide which metals to use in particular applications.

Theories of how creep occurs are even less reliable, and most of our knowledge is still empirical. Creep is a process that is most noticeable in metals under stress and at fairly elevated temperatures. Just what constitutes a fairly elevated temperature varies from metal to metal; the important factor is that at such temperatures lattice faults can move about easily—in a way very similar to that producing recrystallization and stress relaxation. The effect of this is to give a gradual relaxation of stresses by minute slipping of the lattice, and by sliding of individual grains over each other by slow shifting of the grain boundaries. But details of how all this really comes about are still scarce. As with fatigue, metallurgists must still rely on long-term tests—10,000 hours and more—to tell them just how an alloy is liable to behave. And even then the only really reliable information comes from actual service experience.

Typical fatigue fracture. The crack began at the left and progressed slowly across the shaft in easy stages. When the crack had cut the shaft almost halfway through, the remaining metal failed in a typical ductile fracture.

Alloying

So far in this chapter we have been discussing metals without regard to whether they were pure or alloyed. Very few metals are used unalloyed, and it is important to any understanding of metallurgy that the principles upon which alloying is based are understood.

The mechanical behavior of metals depends ultimately upon intimate relationships between ions. If anything happens to alter these relationships, then the behavior of the bulk metal will also be altered. This can be brought about by distortions and movements in the lattice—alterations in spatial relationships—or by changes in the actual ions present. Different pure metals behave differently; when they are mixed together in alloys they might be expected to bring about modifications of one another, because their ions are different sizes, and because they naturally take on different lattice configurations, or, with nonmetallic additions, because they tend to form a different kind of bond. Thus, by controlling alloying the metallurgist can control, within quite close limits, the properties he is aiming at.

Although in practice most alloys contain at least three constituents, and sometimes as many as seven or more, the simplest way of introducing the structure and behavior of metallic alloys is to consider those with only two constituents, so-called *binary* alloys. Most of the basic principles can be studied in this way.

When one attempts to mix two molten metals, one of three main things can happen, depending on the particular metals and on their proportions. First, and especially if a small amount of one metal is added to a much larger amount of another, they may become completely mixed. The smaller amount dissolves in the larger like salt dissolving in water, and the metals are said to be *miscible*. Second, if more of the minority metal is added, a point may be reached beyond which it will no longer dissolve, and the two metals are said to be partially miscible. Third, it occasionally happens that the metals will not dissolve together at all, whatever the proportions of the mix, and the metals are completely immiscible. Such cases as this are quite rare, however; almost all metals dissolve together to at least a small extent, and most combinations are miscible no matter what the proportions.

When alloys solidify, the degree to which they dissolve in one another changes, and usually continues to change as the alloy cools down. At first sight it may seem surprising that we can talk about changes in solubility in solids. When such changes occur in liquids, crystals begin to form; the material whose solubility is falling is forced out of the solution and collects together as crystals. Basically this is also what happens in solid metals; for some reason the lattice can no longer contain as many of the solute ions distributed through it as before, and so they tend to aggregate and form independent crystals. Sometimes these new crystals are not of pure metal, but an alloy of different composition from the mass.

The way in which ions can arrange themselves in alloys varies according to the particular kinds of ions present, two main ways predominating. In the first of these the atoms of the minority metal actually replace atoms of the solvent metal within the lattice, and the crystal structure remains that of the main metal. This sort of solution can be formed only if the atoms of the two metals are similar in size, and take up the same crystal structure. Thus copper and nickel, both face-centered cubic metals, form substitutional solid solutions at all compositions and temperatures.

Substitutional solid solutions behave in very much the same way. as pure metals — and under the microscope they usually look like pure metals. The differences in ionic size affect movements and slip within the lattice, making these movements more difficult, and this produces hardening of the lattice, although the effect is often not very marked. However, some useful hardening can come about if the solute atoms of a substitutional solid solution, of slightly different size from that of the main metal, migrate to the area of dislocations and relieve some of the tension there, making movement of the dislocation more difficult.

The second type of alloy, the interstitial solid solution, is not necessarily always an alloy between metals, but is often between a metal and a nonmetal, such as carbon or nitrogen. In such cases the ions of the nonmetal are small enough to fit in the spaces of the metal lattice, but this can take place to only a limited extent, so that interstitial solid solutions generally consist of only a few parts per cent of nonmetal in a matrix of metal.

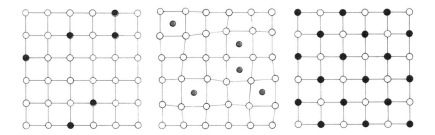

Left: Substitutional solution, with minority ions replacing majority ions at irregular sites in the lattice. Center: Interstitial solution, with minority ions occupying spaces within the distorted lattice of majority ions. Right: Intermetallic compound, where two different metallic ions form a regular lattice in some definite proportion (1 : 1, 1 : 2, 2 : 3, etc.).

Carbon-Steel Alloys

The most common example of an interstitial solution is carbon in iron, which forms the basis of our steel industry. Without the carbon the iron would be uselessly soft, and it would also be impossible to carry out the many heat treatments — case-hardening, tempering, and so on — that make even a simple steel such an extremely versatile material.

The tendency is for iron and carbon to form a covalent compound, iron carbide (cementite), and under certain conditions crystals of this compound do separate out. In other cases the carbon is distributed at random throughout the lattice, and in still others it gathers together as flakes of graphite. All these possibilities can drastically affect the properties of the alloy in which they occur. If we look a little more closely at the way in which these changes can come about, and at their effects, we can get a good idea of some of the ways in which metallurgists make use of alloying to control their materials.

Iron has two crystallographic forms, dependent upon the temperature. Below about 900°C and above 1400°C it is body-centered cubic, while between these temperatures it takes on a face-centered cubic structure. The solubility of carbon in these two structures is different. Face-centered cubic iron will dissolve up to 8·5 atomic per cent (2·0 per cent by weight) of carbon, while body-centered cubic iron will take only a maximum of 0·04 per cent by weight.

The consequences of this variation in solid solubility are interesting and important. Consider a mold of iron containing one quarter per cent weight of carbon, cooling slowly from above its melting temperature down to room temperature. While the mixture is fully molten the carbon is dispersed evenly throughout it. Eventually, at about 1530°C, crystals begin to separate out. At this temperature the iron takes on a body-centered cubic structure, so that these crystals can contain only a small percentage of carbon, the rest remaining in the melt. As the temperature falls and further crystals form, the concentration of carbon in the melt increases, until eventually the temperature is low enough for the iron to solidify in the face-centered cubic structure. At this point two things happen. The iron that has already solidified as the body-centered cubic crystals begins to transform to face-centered cubic. At the same time the remaining liquid solidifies, also in the face-centered cubic structure. Thus the fully solidified metal, known at this stage as *austerite*, now contains crystals with a range of carbon contents from near zero to around one half per cent weight, the average of course being the one quarter per cent weight we started with. This solid solution can now continue to cool in this condition down to about 850°C, when a second transformation begins. Notice that the transformation temperatures are not the same as they would be for pure iron; they vary with composition and, as we shall see later, with rate of cooling. At the moment we are regarding the latter as being so slow that it has no effect.

At 850°C, then, the lattice tends to transform back to body-centered cubic, and in so doing must throw out most of its carbon content. This takes place by gradual diffusion over about 100°C, until eventually the whole matrix has separated out into grains that are almost pure iron (ferrite) and others that consist of laminates of ferrite and of either graphite or iron carbide. The iron carbide is a hard white covalent compound, known as *cementite*, and the grains in which this compound occurs are known as *pearlite*, probably because of their pearly texture when viewed under the microscope.

This structure, which is that of ordinary mild steel, now remains stable during all further cooling. If we reheat the metal the changes are reversed.

Already this has shown us something of the ways in which the properties of a steel might vary simply by variations in its temperature. In the austerite range we have a complete solid solution made up of face-centered cubic crystals, which under the microscope is indistinguishable from pure metal. The widely dispersed carbon tends to inhibit slipping to a certain extent, but not seriously, and the metal is still quite ductile — which, of course, is helped by the fact that the temperature is around 1000°C. Below the lower transformation point we have a quite different state of affairs. Here we usually have hard brittle laminates of cementite, which form effective barriers to dislocation movement, surrounded by a ductile matrix of almost pure iron. It is this combination that gives mild steel much of its toughness.

Variations in this state of affairs can be brought about, as we have already suggested, by variations in the composition and in the rate of cooling, and also by the use of varied cooling and heating cycles. Let us look at these in turn.

If we increase the carbon content to between 0·8 and about 2·0 per cent (the limit of carbon solubility in FCC iron), then we shall not get the higher body-centered cubic state; instead the melt solidifies straight away as face-centered cubic crystals of austerite. As we cool this down we find another change in the sequence, for at some temperature between 1130°C and 720°C, depending on the carbon content — the higher temperature applying to the greater proportion of carbon — cementite begins to separate out, leaving behind austerite of increasingly lower carbon content. When the temperature reaches 720°C we have a matrix of austerite containing 0·8 per cent carbon surrounding a quantity of cementite that depends upon the average carbon content of the steel. At 720°C the austerite undergoes a rapid transformation to body-centered cubic ferrite and pearlite. This is the type of steel known simply as *high-carbon* steel, used as the basis for many high-strength engineering steels.

Beyond 2·0 per cent carbon, austerite cannot take all the carbon present into solution, whatever the temperature, and cementite

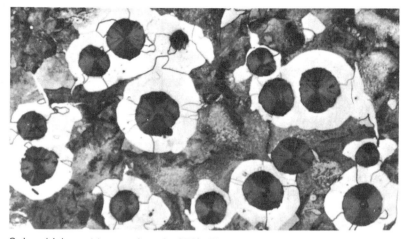

Spheroidal graphite cast iron (×250). The dark areas are carbon (graphite), the white areas iron carbide (cementite), and the light grey background is iron containing a small percentage of dissolved carbon.

begins to separate out as soon as the melt solidifies. Once again what austerite there is transforms to ferrite and pearlite at 720°C. Irons with such a carbon content are known as cast irons. They are characterized by their brittleness, which arises from the large proportions of cementite, and which makes them quite unsuited to fabrication by forging.

By increasing the rate of cooling we can modify these changes still more, the most important effect being a suppression of the temperature of the austerite-ferrite transformation. This is a super-cooling effect, so that when the transformation does eventually take place it pushes the carbon out of solution more quickly than at lower cooling rates. The result is that the carbon ions do not diffuse far enough to form as large aggregates, and thus the pearlite has a much finer texture. As the cooling rate is increased, therefore, the pearlite takes on an increasingly fine texture, and in these conditions is given the name *sorbite*, and, when very fine, *troostite*. Eventually, if the steel or iron is quenched in cold water from high in the austerite range, the cooling rate is high enough, except at very low carbon contents, to affect the transformation in a quite different way. Now the carbon does not have time to come out of solution at all, for the rate at which it can move about the lattice is too slow. The result is a highly distorted body-centered cubic lattice, known as *martensite*, which is extremely hard, and somewhat brittle.

This transformation is one of the most important in the whole of ferrous metallurgy, for it provides us with a simple technique for producing tough, hard steels. The simplest example of its use is that of case hardening of, say, automobile gears. The starting point for this is a mild steel, usually containing fractions of a per cent of chromium and perhaps nickel, which go into substitutional solid solution and so give some toughening and slight modification of the transformations. We can ignore these last in the present argument.

The carbon content of the steel is such that if we water-quench, a thin martensite layer may be formed at the surface, but its thickness and hardness are not sufficient to give the wear-resistance we are seeking. Below the surface the cooling rate is too low to produce a martensite transformation at all.

When case hardening, we simply increase the carbon content of the metal surface layers by holding the metal in the austerite range in contact with some source of carbon such as coke or a gas that decomposes to deposit carbon, e.g. carbon tetrachloride, CCl_4. Then when we quench in water we get a hard martensite skin backed by a tough core of increasingly coarse pearlite steel. We must be careful not to increase the carbon content too much, for as we approach two per cent we may find that the martensite contains soft grains of untransformed austerite.

Very strong steels can be made by quenching in such a way that the steel transforms completely to martensite, and then heating it to around 100–150°C for, say, an hour, so that some of the more intense internal stresses are relieved. To produce such *through-hardened* steels, as they are called, it is necessary to make other alloying additions, particularly nickel, which reduce the cooling rate needed to produce the martensite transformation.

Another important heat treatment based on the production of martensite is that in which the steel is held at 350–400°C for a while, when the martensite gradually relaxes as carbon comes out of solution. The result is the formation of troostite or sorbite, the tough, fine-grained versions of pearlite. These forms are best produced in this way rather than by direct quenching, for in the latter they are very difficult to produce alone, being generally mixed up with more or less martensite.

Age Hardening

In discussing martensite, we saw that by cooling an alloy very rapidly it is possible to prevent a constituent from coming out of solution even when, considering its normal solubility, it should apparently do so. This is true not just of steels, but also of many other alloys, and in some cases the effect can be used to give a type of hardening called *age hardening* or *precipitation hardening*. A good example of this is the aluminum alloy Duralumin and its derivatives, widely used in the aircraft industry.

In 1909 a German metallurgist, Dr. Alfred Wilm, was trying to develop stronger aluminum alloys, so that these very light materials might be used in aircraft. One of the alloys he tried contained 4 per cent of copper and 0·5 per cent each of manganese and magnesium. The first tests showed this to be unsuccessful, the additions giving only a small amount of strengthening. A few days later there arose some doubt about the accuracy of the first tests and the samples were tested again. They were found to be almost half as strong again as had been expected — 28 tons per square inch instead of about 20 tons per square inch. Obviously this was no simple experimental error, and Wilm started a series of tests to show the effects of storing alloys for various lengths of time after manufacture. These showed that such strengths could be reached consistently if the alloy was heated to 500°C for a while, quenched, then left for a few days at room temperature. The new alloy was given the name Duralumin after the Durener Metallwerke at Duren, in which Wilm worked. Count Zeppelin used it successfully in the construction of his famous airships, and Duralumin was soon used by all the leading aircraft manufacturers. Today alloys descended from this original age-hardening aluminum alloy form the structure and covering of almost every aircraft.

The phenomenon is actually quite complex in operation, and no complete explanation has yet been evolved, but we can get some idea from the previous concepts in this chapter. When the solid

54

Stages in precipitation hardening. In the first diagram, the minority ions are dispersed throughout the lattice, and do not contribute much hardening. In the center diagram, the minority ions have collected and are straining the lattice by imposing their own lattice size. This is the point of maximum hardness. At the far right, the minority ions have broken loose from the lattice and have little effect. The alloy is " overaged."

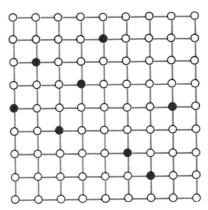

alloy is at 500°C, all the copper is in substitutional solid solution. (The magnesium and manganese also play a part, but they are much less important than the copper; we shall ignore them in this discussion.) At room temperature the solid solubility of copper in aluminum falls to less than 0·5 per cent weight, so that if we quench the alloy in water we form an unstable lattice supersaturated with copper. Unlike martensite, however, this lattice, having undergone no transformation and containing no interstitial constituents, is not particularly distorted or hardened by the treatment.

After a time the solute in unstable solution begins to agglomerate into what will eventually be a separate, undissolved phase. In some alloys this can happen quite quickly — a matter of a very few hours — at room temperature. In the more important practical cases it is necessary to heat the alloy to a few hundred degrees — although not to anywhere near the temperature at which the solution becomes stable — in order to bring about the effect.

The diagram shows what happens as this agglomeration proceeds. At first the gathering ions form a lattice that is coherent with the main lattice. To do this it must produce distortions that extend over quite a large distance. These distortions hinder dislocation movement in the lattice, and so produce hardening. With more time these precipitates become independent of the main lattice (they are now said to be incoherent) and the distortion they cause is greatly reduced. The alloy has now reached a fairly stable state with the excess solute completely out of solution. Complete stability is

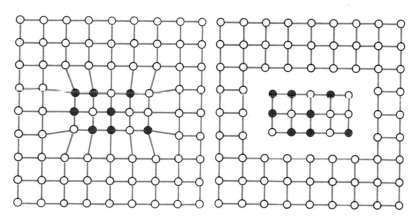

reached when many of the incoherent particles have migrated together, and again the metal is relatively soft, the distance between particles being too great and their lattice distortion effect too small to cause appreciable hardening.

It is obvious from all this that the most useful point in this process is just before the coherent precipitate becomes incoherent. Thus the lattice distortion is greatest, and the hardening effect most intense. Beyond this point the alloy softens again, and is said to be *overaged*. In alloys in which the solute atoms can move about fairly easily at room temperature, overaging cannot be avoided. Thus the best alloys from this point of view are those in which the coherent precipitate is formed at an elevated temperature. Then, by quenching the alloy at the right moment (found by experience) the process can be halted at its most effective point. Age hardening is now probably the most common way of strengthening alloys. It is used not only for alloys to be employed at ordinary temperatures, such as aluminum alloys, copper-beryllium, and high-strength steels, but also for alloys to be used at quite high temperatures. We shall be discussing these alloys in Chapter 5.

3 The Extraction of Metals

The production of pure metal from an ore is no longer a matter for the empirical craftsman, as it was over so many centuries; it has become a sophisticated branch of chemical engineering, making as full as possible a use of our knowledge of chemistry and of thermodynamics. In many cases the techniques that have been evolved empirically are still used, with only modifications of equipment and methods based on our modern scientific knowledge. But in other cases the problems of the extraction and refining of metals are being approached afresh. Using basic theoretical principles, completely new and more effective methods are being developed, either to produce traditional metals more cheaply, or for the extraction of metals that were previously prohibitively expensive.

Even though a metal may occur naturally in some extremely complex mineral, and in very small concentrations, there are few instances where we do not have sufficient knowledge of chemistry to allow us to extract and refine it. This is not the main point,

Molten iron, brought direct from the blast furnace in the ladle, being cast into " pigs," or ingots.

however; we must be able to obtain the pure metal economically. Thus the aim of any sequence of operations that we may design must be to produce the required metal with an overall expenditure of materials and energy compatible with its market value.

The first requirement is a mineral deposit of such a composition, and in such a location, that we can develop an economic extraction process for it. As much as possible of the unwanted rock, the *gangue*, is removed by physical processing at the minehead, so that only what is absolutely necessary is transported to the extraction and refining plant. Once at the latter, the ore—any metallic mineral sufficiently rich for extraction is known as an ore—is first converted into a form suitable for feeding into the smelting furnaces. As we shall see later, the naturally occurring chemical form of a mineral may not be the aptest for direct conversion into metal, and so the process is split into two stages, beginning with a conversion from, say, sulfide or carbonate, to, say, the metal oxide. Also, the physical form may be unsatisfactory. During physical separation at the minehead—known generally as *comminution* and *concentration*—the mineral is reduced to a fairly fine powder or slurry, which, if fed into a smelting furnace, would simply fuse into an intractable mass, or block up any gas lines there might be. To overcome such difficulties the finely ground ore is reformed into lumps or pellets by heating to a temperature of a few hundred degrees—a process known as *sintering*. Often this is combined with preliminary chemical conversion, and sometimes fuel, for a later stage, such as coke, is incorporated here also.

Conversion of the sintered mineral to metal needs an input of energy—that is, it needs fuel, which may be chemical or electrical, the exact form used depending on the chemical nature of the mineral, or on the location of the extraction plant, or both. And the metal thus produced will generally need to be refined before it can be fabricated and put to good use. Depending upon the needs of the final application, impurities have to be removed to a given standard. These impurities consist of particles of waste rock, of fragments picked up from the furnace lining, or of dissolved gases. Once again energy for this must be provided from chemical or electrical fuel.

This outlines the main stages common to all metal extraction — the selection of an ore, its preparation for smelting, and then the actual smelting and refining processes. Each one of these depends upon the others, and naturally the details vary from metal to metal, from ore to ore, and from plant to plant. There are basic principles common to all, however, and it is these that we shall be examining in this chapter, with illustrations drawn from actual cases.

Ore as it is mined consists of an intimate mixture of metallic mineral and unwanted material such as clay or rock, known generally as *gangue*. The mineral contains the metal in chemical combination with one or more other elements such as oxygen, sulfur, carbon, silicon, chlorine, or fluorine, the first two being by far the most common. Such minerals are spread widely throughout the earth's crust, but generally thinly. Only in certain areas have they become concentrated enough, through the action of the weather or, more usually, through geological changes, to form potential ore-fields. Differences in chemical composition from place to place are also important in determining whether a concentration of mineral can be regarded as an ore, and these too can be traced to changes in geological conditions and to weathering effects. Aluminum, for instance, is one of the most common metals present in the earth's crust. Most of this is locked up in clay as complex silicates, however, for which as yet there is no economic extraction process. Only in certain limited areas, such as the Caribbean, is aluminum found as a simple oxide, which can be much more readily reduced to the pure metal.

Cleaning and Roasting the Ore

The processing of ore to produce metal, then, breaks down into two main sections. First, there is the removal of the gangue. This is not attached chemically to the metal, and thus is removed largely by physical processes. Second, the mineral itself must be treated chemically to part the metal from its associated elements. We shall look at these two stages in turn.

Physical removal of gangue has three main functions. Its prime function, naturally, is to get rid of useless material. A secondary function is to reduce the cost of transporting ore from the mine to the smelters, which may be anything up to several thousand miles

Iron
Nickel
Copper

Major world sources of ore for the metals indicated.

Aluminum
Titanium
Zinc

away. For instance, bauxite—aluminum oxide—mined in the Caribbean, must be shipped through the Panama Canal and up the west coast of America to British Columbia, where there is a supply of cheap hydroelectricity for smelting. Third, the removal of gangue before the mineral is fed to the smelters avoids complications during chemical processing. For any gangue that does find its way into the smelters must be gathered up by the action of slag; and if no attempt was made to remove gangue before this stage, vast amounts of slag would have to be used, greatly increasing the complication and cost of smelting, and with a very good chance of the final metal containing a high percentage of trapped impurities, thus adding to the refining costs. By removing gangue at the mine, we are in fact helping to cut the cost of the later refining processes. The later refining processes tend to be expensive because they need large supplies of energy, in the form of heat or electricity, to help break the strong chemical bonds of the mineral, unlike the physical processes of gangue removal we shall discuss, which may be very simple and need little energy.

Mineral and gangue cannot be separated while they are still mixed together in the large ore lumps that usually come out of a mine. Thus the first thing we must do is to break the ore down to a fine powder by crushing and then grinding it. This comminution process has the effect of ensuring that each particle of the powder is either wholly mineral or wholly gangue. The partition is rarely perfect, but it is enough to ensure that when we come to separate the two components, very little gangue is passed on to the smelters, and very little metal is lost in the discarded gangue.

There are a great many techniques for separating the powdered mineral from the powdered gangue—concentrating the ore—but all of them exploit the different physical characteristics of the two different types of particle. Thus if the two have reasonably different densities, floating them in a liquid of intermediate density will ensure that the lighter component can be skimmed off at the top while the heavy component sinks. Again, if the metal is magnetic, then we can pass the powder along a continuous electromagnetic belt so designed that the gangue falls off the end, while the mineral is carried on, to be dropped at will at some point where the magnetic field is cut off. The most important technique, however,

62

is froth flotation, in which one or other of the components is selectively floated off on the bubbles of an intense froth. The selection is made possible by treating the powdered ore, suspended in water, with a chemical similar to a detergent, which affects the surface of the mineral in such a way that it adheres easily to the froth, formed by a second chemical, the frothing agent. The process can be very selective, allowing the separation of different minerals, as well as minerals from gangue. Copper and nickel, for instance, are often found together in complex mixed ores of copper sulfide and nickel sulfide, along with some iron, and traces of gold, silver, platinum, and other precious metals. Early in the processing the mineral particles are treated by flotation and are separated into three concentrates, one rich in copper, another rich in nickel, and a third rich in iron. This is done entirely by careful use of the right chemicals to give selective flotation.

Before the concentrated mineral particles can be smelted they must often be put through a preliminary roasting process; this involves exposing them to the air or controlled atmosphere at

Treatment of copper-nickel ore at the mine head. The larger chunks, richer in metal, are treated by crushing (1), grinding (2), flotation (3), and magnetic separation (4) ; the tailings are discarded (5), the concentrated ore (6) goes to further processing. The finely divided and leaner ore is agglomerated (7), undergoes preliminary smelting (8), the gangue is discarded as slag (9) and the concentrate (10) goes for processing.

temperatures up to 1000°c or more, which, while not causing them to melt, brings about changes that put the mineral in a suitable condition for smelting. The precise object of roasting varies with different ores. Zinc sulfide, for instance, may be roasted in an atmosphere with a high sulfur dioxide and oxygen content to produce zinc sulfate (suitable for the production of zinc by electrolysis), or at higher temperature in air to produce sulfur-free zinc oxide, which can be reduced to zinc by carbon monoxide. Iron oxide minerals, on the other hand, are roasted in such a way that they agglomerate into porous lumps suitable for feeding to the blast furnace, chemical reactions at this stage being of secondary importance. Carbonates and sulfates of various metals are roasted to convert them to oxides.

The aim of all these preliminaries is to increase the ease with which we can bring about the eventual chemical separation of the metal. They have all been aimed at producing the mineral in a simple form, from which we can eventually separate the combined metal by the application of energy of a suitable kind.

Ore Reduction Techniques

In the previous chapter we saw how metals tend to combine with nonmetals by exchange of valency electrons to form ionic compounds. In discussing metal extraction we are discussing the formation and dissolution of these compounds; our aim is to reverse the electron exchange and thus to separate the components. There are four ways in which we can do this. The choice depends on the stability of the particular compounds involved, as well as on the type of fuel (or energy source) most readily available.

The first of these is simple heating, used in those cases where the compound is relatively unstable. Metals are rarely found naturally in such a state that this technique can be used on them directly, but it often forms a final stage in the extraction of metals such as gold or the platinum metals from the very complex compounds in which they are often found (if they are not in their raw state, as is quite commonly the case, especially with gold). Silver, copper, and mercury, which may also be found in their raw state but are more commonly found combined with oxygen or sulfur, can be produced by heating their compounds to around 400°c. With more reactive compounds the problem becomes more difficult; the amount of energy, and hence the necessary heating temperature, becomes greater as the metals become more reactive, and we soon begin to reach limits set by our heat-producing facilities and the problems of furnace construction.

Stability of Metallic Compounds

Fortunately, there are other ways of obtaining a metal from its oxide or sulfide than simple heating. One of them is to place the oxide in contact with a different metal and allow the two to react, when the unwanted oxygen transfers from one metal to the other. For instance, titanium oxide and aluminum metal will, under suitable conditions, turn into titanium metal and aluminum oxide; the aluminum has been *oxidized*, while the titanium oxide has been *reduced*. Hence we can produce titanium from its oxide using aluminum as a reducing agent.

The fact that oxygen leaves the titanium and goes over to the aluminum means that it must have a greater affinity for the one metal than it has for the other; obviously, if we wanted to produce aluminum from its oxide we could not use titanium as the reducing agent. Clearly it is important to know which metals have a great affinity for oxygen — these form oxides which are very stable — and which metals have little affinity. The former will be good reducing agents for oxides of the latter but their own oxides will be hard to reduce.

What determines the stability of a chemical compound? We have seen in Chapter 1 that a physical system is most stable when its energy is as low as it can get. Whether or not several atoms will form a compound when brought together therefore depends on whether they can lose some of their energy by doing so. Imagine two atoms being brought together slowly. The charged particles in each atom gradually experience forces due to the electrostatic and electromagnetic fields produced by the other atom. In many cases, as when the atoms are both of oxygen, it is possible for the electrons to rearrange themselves in such a way that their total energy is reduced, and in the new arrangement a few electrons will be moving in orbits that are not associated with one atom or the other but that cover both of them. Because the energy is lower in this

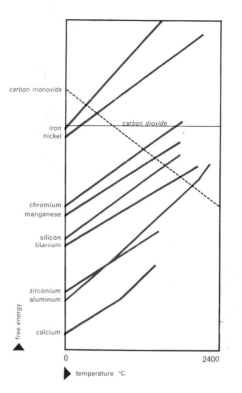

Relative stability of metallic oxides (and carbon monoxide and dioxide) as a function of temperature. At a given temperature, any metal will reduce (i.e. remove oxygen from) the oxides of metals above it; alternatively, its oxide will be reduced by metals below it.

arrangement, two oxygen atoms always form a stable molecule (O_2) and it would require a very large input of energy to dissociate an oxygen molecule. Similar considerations apply to any chemical reaction. They all involve the rearrangement of atoms into new kinds of molecules, and the reaction will proceed in the direction that represents a net lowering of the internal energies of the molecules. When calcium reacts with oxygen, for instance, there must be some energy supplied to break the bonds holding the calcium atoms in place in the metal crystal, and to break the bond between the two oxygen atoms in a molecule, but there is considerably more energy released by the formation of calcium oxide (CaO). The net result is increased chemical stability and the release of heat, called the heat of reaction, which represents the excess energy. Calcium therefore has a strong affinity for oxygen.

The heat of reaction is only a rough measure of the readiness of chemicals to react, and there are some complicated factors involved in the energy changes during a reaction about which we have said nothing. A molecule can possess internal energy besides that of its electrons; for instance, in the form of vibrations of the atoms or rotations of the whole molecule. Also, reactions often involve changes of volume in which energy is expended or absorbed. The true measure of the readiness of a reaction to occur is provided by the thermodynamic function called the free energy. What is important is the difference between the free energy of the compounds we start with and those we are trying to form.

The diagram on page 65 shows the free energy, as a function of temperature, for a number of reactions between metals and oxygen to form oxides. Also included are the reactions between carbon and oxygen to give, in one case, carbon monoxide, in the other, carbon dioxide. The lower down in the diagram the metal is, the more stable its oxide. Thus the oxide of a metal can be reduced by any other metal that appears lower down; calcium could be used to reduce the oxide of any other metal in the diagram, though whether this is an economic process is another matter. Similar graphs can be drawn for any reaction or group of reactions.

Free energy depends on temperature, and we can see from the graph that it increases with temperature for all the metals. Thus, the affinity of metals for oxygen decreases as the temperature rises, and we already know that any metallic oxide can, in principle, be decomposed by heating it strongly enough. Where two lines in the diagram cross, the relative stability of the oxides is reversed, so that aluminum reduces zirconium oxide at low temperatures, but the reaction goes the other way at high ones.

The importance of the carbon graphs is now clear. They do not rise with temperature, at least, not in the region covered by the diagram, which goes beyond the range of ordinary commercial furnaces. One of the carbon lines, in fact, slopes downward. This means that we can use carbon as a reducing agent for any metal oxide as long as the temperature is high enough, which in many cases means a much lower temperature than would be necessary to decompose it by heat alone. Carbon is readily available as a reducing agent in the form of coke, charcoal, coal, or oil. Carbon

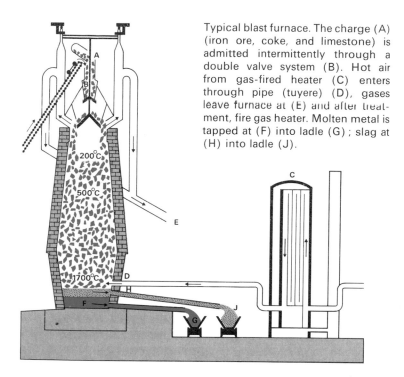

Typical blast furnace. The charge (A) (iron ore, coke, and limestone) is admitted intermittently through a double valve system (B). Hot air from gas-fired heater (C) enters through pipe (tuyere) (D), gases leave furnace at (E) and after treatment, fire gas heater. Molten metal is tapped at (F) into ladle (G); slag at (H) into ladle (J).

monoxide is also a good reducing agent in the reaction in which it forms carbon dioxide, and this is useful because, being a gas, it can be brought into intimate contact with solid oxides. This applies particularly to the smelting of iron and zinc. We shall look at the smelting of iron in more detail.

The modern blast furnace, in which the process takes place, is in effect a 200-foot-high truncated iron cone, lined with refractory bricks, with a 25-foot-diameter hearth at the bottom. It can turn out 2000 tons or more of iron every day, stopping only every two or three years, for a new lining and general cleanup.

Dressed, and sintered ore, coke, and sand or limestone flux are fed through a double-bell gas-lock system at the top, while a hot blast of air is blown in through tuyeres around the sides a few feet above the hearth. Every few hours the furnace crew open up holes in the bottom of the furnace, allowing first a slag containing many of the impurities, such as residual gangue, to run off, and then the molten iron at around 1600°C.

Basically the reactions that take place to produce the iron from iron oxide sinter are simple. The coke, almost pure carbon, reacts with the oxygen from the air blast, forming carbon monoxide. As this passes up the furnace it reduces the iron oxide, producing iron and carbon dioxide. The heat from the reaction of the coke and air is sufficient to melt the iron, which flows gradually down into the hearth, being scavenged (cleansed) of the worst of its impurities by the lime or sand as it does so.

Unfortunately carbon or carbon monoxide reduction, although quite a cheap method, cannot be used with every ore. The more reactive metals like aluminum and magnesium would need high temperatures that are difficult or expensive to achieve, and that in any case would vaporize the metal. Again, metals in ores are not always conveniently combined with oxygen or with some element easily replaced by oxygen. Also, an ore might be quite a complex one—platinum ore, for instance—demanding long and expensive

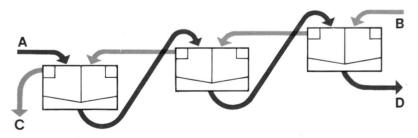

Above: Countercurrent decantation. The slurry or pulp (A) is drawn from the bottom of each vat and pumped to the vat at right. The liquid (B) in which the desired mineral is dissolved is drawn from the top of each vat to the vat at left, and leaves at (C). Right: Part of a complex leaching plant separating the six platinum-type metals as well as silver and gold.

smelting processes. In such cases, the extraction metallurgist will have to try a different approach.

One such approach is *leaching*, a process in which a suitable dilute acid or alkali is used in order to dissolve the valuable mineral out of the ore. For instance, in one method of producing zinc from zinc-sulfide ore, the ore is first roasted, as we saw earlier, to produce a zinc sulfate. This is then leached with dilute sulfuric acid, the mineral being dissolved and the insoluble gangue being left behind. The result is an acidic solution of zinc sulfate. We shall see in a moment how we can then extract the zinc.

Leaching reactions are usually much faster even at ordinary temperatures than the reactions involved in smelting, and thus the actual process temperatures may be quite low—say 60 or 70°C, as compared to about 1800°C in smelting iron. If it *is* necessary to speed up the reactions, this can sometimes be done on the " pressure cooker " principle, where high pressures, often many times greater than atmospheric pressure, prevent superheated liquids from boiling.

Once the metal has been dissolved away from the gangue, there is still the problem of removing it from the solution. One way of doing this is to use simple displacement similar to the reduction methods we have already described. Just as with metals and oxides, there is a scale, some metals being more easily displaced from solution than others. Thus gold, which is very difficult to dissolve, is easily displaced by almost any other metal. Zinc, on the other hand, dissolves quite easily, and only a very reactive metal such as sodium or magnesium could be used to displace it. In some cases, for instance in the production of nickel by leaching with ammonia, hydrogen is used instead of metal as the reducing agent.

In another method the metal is displaced not as a pure metal but as a simple compound—an oxide, for instance. Because the compound is free from gangue, it is fairly easy to reduce to metal by smelting in the ordinary way.

Our third main method for recovering metal from a leach solution is to use electrical energy. When an ionic compound dissolves, its ions separate and lead independent lives within the solution, which will pass electric current and is known as an electrolyte. If we put two electrodes in an electrolyte and apply a voltage across them, the negatively charged ions will be drawn toward the positive electrode. There they will give up their surplus electrons and form neutral atoms or molecules again, usually of gases such as oxygen or chlorine, depending on the type of solution. The electrons they have given up then pass around the outside circuit to the negative electrode, where they meet and neutralize the positively charged metal ions that have been drawn to it. These ions then become neutral atoms of metal and are deposited on the electrode. The whole process is called *electrolysis*. Thus we have brought about the desired redistribution of electrons by the application of electrical energy. This is the method used to extract the zinc from the zinc sulfate we produced a few pages ago.

Electrolysis is generally a more efficient method than the two displacement techniques, as it produces a very pure metal, but the cost of electricity often makes it too expensive. Electrolysis is not used directly on the leach solution of very reactive metals such as aluminum or magnesium, but on some molten compound of the metal displaced from the solution by other means.

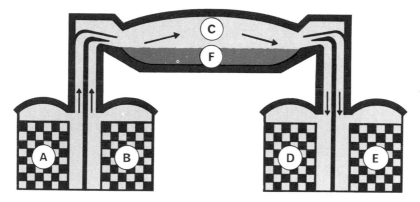

Open-hearth steel furnace. Fuel gas is blown in through hot brickwork at (A), air through hot brickwork at (B). The gas burns at (C), the exhaust gases heat the brickwork at (D) and (E). As the regenerators (A and B) cool, the flow is reversed, and (D) and (E) do the preheating of the gases. The charge (F) is composed of pig iron, steel scrap, slagging additions, and iron ore (as an oxygen source).

Refining Techniques

Electrolysis apart, the other processes described so far have all been designed to produce the metal in a fairly crude form. In most cases we must treat this metal further to reduce the impurities to a level that engineers, builders, and other users will accept. These further processes are known as *refining* processes.

The impurities in crude metal take many forms. They may be other metals or nonmetals that have become either dissolved or trapped in the main metal during smelting. They may originate from the atmosphere or from other minerals in the ore. They may have crept in from the fuels, the fluxes, or the furnace linings in the plant itself. Whatever their origin, such impurities usually make the metal less useful; they reduce its strength, for instance, or its hardness. Sometimes, too, impurities may be quite valuable in their own right; for example, precious metals like gold, silver, platinum, iridium, and others found in copper, nickel, and lead.

In terms of sheer quantity, fire-refining is probably the most important method, although it is by no means the most effective. Examples are the Bessemer, LD, and open-hearth processes for converting pig iron into steel, and the fire-refining techniques sometimes used for copper and lead. Common to all of them is the use of oxygen (either pure, or in air, or in compounds in the ore itself) to combine with and carry away the unwanted materials into the slag. Obviously, then, they are useful only where the metal being refined has a lower affinity for oxygen than the elements

Opposite: Stages in the Linz-Donowitz oxygen steel-making process. In (1) the vessel contains some slag from the previous batch, to which steel scrap (2) and then molten pig iron are added (3). Oxygen (and lime powder) are blown in (4), burning out carbon and phosphorus. The slag is then poured off (5) and additional alloying components may be added. The oxygen lance is then returned for further burning out of undesired elements (6). The charge is then decanted (7) and the vessel is ready for the next batch (8).

Below: The Linz-Donowitz process in operation. The photo corresponds to step 4 at left.

74

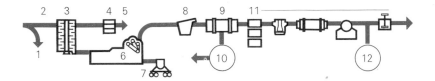

Flow chart for copper-nickel concentrate refining. Iron-rich nickel concentrate (1) has been separated magnetically for other processing. The copper-containing nickel sulfide (2) is roasted (3), metal in the exhaust gas is recovered by electrostatic precipitation (4) ; the gas (5) is reused. The roasted ore is melted in a reverberatory furnace (6), slag is discarded (7), the molten copper-nickel sulfide (8) is blown with air in a Bessemer converter (9) removing all iron in the slag (10). The concentrate is cooled slowly (11), giving copper sulfide crystals, nickel sulfide crystals, and a copper-nickel alloy containing precious metals (silver, gold, platinum, etc.). The precious metals concentrate (12) and the copper sulfide concentrate (13) are separated by crushing, grinding, magnetic separation, and flotation. The nickel sulfide concentrate (14) is sintered (15) to nickel oxide (16) and marketed as such for steel alloying. Alternatively, the nickel sulfide may be oxidized to nickel oxide by fluid bed roasting (17). The oxide (18), reduced (19) and volatilized (20) as nickel carbonyl gas (21), decomposes (22) to pure nickel

being removed. This means that fire-refining is useless for active metals such as aluminum and magnesium.

As we have seen, electrolysis gives a fairly pure metal from leach solutions. Not surprisingly, then, the same process is an important way of refining crude metals. In this case, the crude metal is formed into a lump and used as the positive electrode, or *anode*, in an acid or alkaline solution of the same metal. As the current passes, both the anode and some of the metallic impurities it contains dissolve into the electrolyte. Those impurities that do not dissolve either collect as a sludge on the bottom of the tank or remain attached to the anode. The purification relies on the fact that ions of different metals need different electric voltages before they begin to " plate out " onto the negative electrode, or *cathode*. Thus, by carefully selecting the voltage, the unwanted one is deposited on the cathode, from which it can then be stripped. The metals commonly refined in this way are copper, nickel, and cobalt, but the method can also be used for refining zinc, tin, and several other metals.

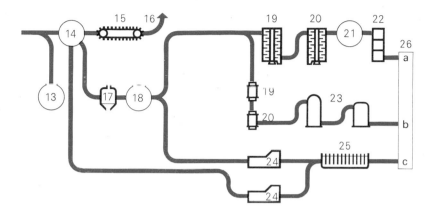

pellets (26a) and carbon monoxide, which is recycled. Alternatively, the nickel carbonyl gas may be fractionally distilled (23), and decomposed to nickel powder (26b). Finally, either the sulfide or the oxide may be melted in reverberatory furnaces (24) and electrolytically refined (25) to produce pure nickel cathodes, or ingots (26c). The by-products include thirteen different elements, mostly metals in varying degrees of purity and separation.

One consequence of the vast progress of technology over the past 20 years has been the increase in the need for precise control to a hitherto unprecedented degree. The success of a new process or the safety of a project such as a space shot depend on the maintenance of very great accuracies, both in the making of components and in the way they work. Inevitably these demands have been felt in the metals industry just as much as anywhere else, not only in the shaping processes but in the actual manufacture of metals and alloys. Two decades ago, metals with impurity levels of only a few parts per million would have been called ultrapure; today, when materials are being pushed to the very limits of endurance, they could cause disastrous failures. Operating temperatures are becoming more and more extreme at both ends of the scale; parts of a rocket engine may reach punishing temperatures of four or five thousand degrees c, while the new supermagnets being made must be kept around $-270°$c, which is about as cold as it is possible to get. Stresses continue to rise; some machines—giant excavators, for instance—call for components that can carry upward of 100 tons per square inch. In such conditions the possibilities of fatigue and fracture under a sudden increase in load become major headaches for the designer. Even the radio set makes exacting demands. Transistors, for instance, are actually crystals of semi-conducting material that contain deliberate impurities (by varying the impurities we change the functioning of the transistor), and these impurities must be controlled to within one part in 10 million.

To meet these demands, metallurgists have developed a whole new range of refining techniques, far surpassing the achievements of the traditional methods.

The first thing they realized when they were developing these new techniques was that the last stages of refining and alloying could no longer be carried out in air. One of the most persistent sources of impurity has always been the atmosphere, from which molten metals pick up and trap various gases. To avoid this, melting would have to be under vacuum. Other sources of impurity during melting are the fuel and the furnace lining. The obvious answer to the first was to do away completely with direct contact between the fuel and the metal. Wherever manufacturers set out to make ultrapure metals, they have adopted electrical furnace-heating techniques. The lining presented more difficult problems.

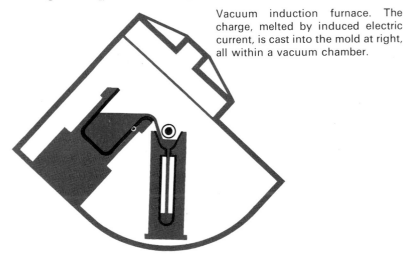

Vacuum induction furnace. The charge, melted by induced electric current, is cast into the mold at right, all within a vacuum chamber.

Most furnaces are lined with special refractory bricks that can withstand high temperatures without melting or becoming weakened. But often small fragments flake off from the bricks, and these, together with gas and moisture released from them, are picked up by the metal and can become a quite serious source of impurity. Most vacuum refining furnaces now have copper linings, water-cooled to prevent them from melting when they are in contact with metal that may often be several hundred degrees hotter than 1083°C, the melting point of the copper.

Unlike traditional processes, refining under vacuum does away with the need for any slagging additions; in fact if this was not so, there would be no point in going to the trouble of producing a vacuum, for the process would defeat itself by allowing impurities to be picked up from the slag. However, under vacuum any gas content that the metal might have had is drawn out, while inclusions of nonmetals are removed by becoming vaporized. The result is an exceptionally " clean " material.

Which Extraction Process?

We have now covered some of the basic ideas and techniques used in the extraction of metals. Usually no one method is immediately obvious as the way of extracting a particular metal, but

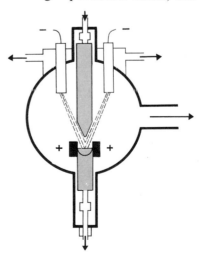

Electron-beam refining. Metal to be refined (pink) is fed into a vacuum chamber, vaporized by the converging electron beam, and swept to the anode. The impurities are removed by the vacuum pump.

in practice a whole range of metallurgical, engineering, and economic factors combine to make one or two methods predominant.

In the first place, as we have seen, the choice depends on the type of ore—that is, on the other elements the metal is combined with and the type and proportion of gangue from which it must be separated. The impurities in the gangue are particularly important; even a rich ore may be completely useless if it contains a very small proportion of some element that is particularly difficult to remove.

Engineering difficulties may arise if a process calls for very high temperatures. This is not so much because of the sheer difficulty of producing such temperatures (though that *is* difficult), but rather because of the problems involved in building equipment to withstand them for long periods. Also, if the metal itself, or any of the elements associated with it, is particularly reactive when hot, then the costs of making suitable containers, such as effective furnace linings, could well be prohibitive.

Economics of Metal Extraction

Even so, such technical problems, however simple or complex they may be, are always overshadowed by economics. Chemists in their laboratories can probably extract anything from anything—at a price. But industrial processes must take account of

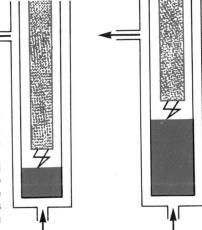

Consumable-arc refining. The metal to be refined, in a vacuum chamber, is used as one electrode of an electric arc ; the molten metal (from the arc) is the other electrode. Vaporized impurities are swept away by the vacuum system, and the entire chamber is cooled by continuous flow of water in the surrounding water jacket.

market values; if a metal brings a low price, then extraction processes must be cheap; if it has a high value, more money can be spent on its production. The value of by-products is also important. Nickel, for instance, is produced from ores in which it forms only 1–2 per cent of the total; but from the same ore come copper, iron, cobalt, gold, silver, platinum, palladium, rhodium, ruthenium, iridium, selenium, tellurium, and sulfur.

If a deposit of low-grade ore is near to transport facilities, and perhaps also near to fuel so that it can be smelted on the spot, then it will often be cheaper to exploit than a much richer deposit that is less accessible. A mountain of rich iron ore (containing, say, 60 per cent iron) in the heart of the Brazilian jungle would probably not be mined because of the immense cost of moving equipment to it, and of bringing the mined ore out to the furnaces. On the other hand, the iron ores used in England are among the poorest in the world, with iron contents often below 25 per cent, but they are close to transport, coal or coke, good supplies of limestone and sand, and to the places where the iron will be used.

Thus we see that at every stage of mining, dressing, roasting, smelting, and refining, the producers must ask themselves: " How much will this cost? " and " How much will it raise the value of the finished metal? "

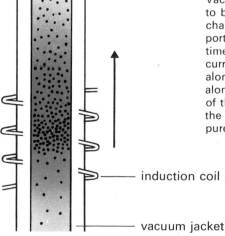

Vacuum-zone refining. The metal bar to be refined is placed in a vacuum chamber. The heating coil melts a portion or " zone " of the bar at a time, by electrically inducing eddy currents in the bar. As the coil moves along the bar, impurities are swept along in the molten zone, to one end of the bar. Repeated applications of the process have resulted in metals pure to less than 1 part in a million.

induction coil

vacuum jacket

4 The Shaping of Metals

The usefulness of metals depends not only on their properties in the final metal object, but also on the relative ease with which they may be brought to this final useful shape. The conventional metal-shaping processes depend ultimately on the ductility of metals or on their not-unreasonably-high melting points. In some of the modern alloys developed for particularly arduous service these agreeable characteristics of metals are lost, and we must resort to other techniques to be described in a later chapter.

Methods

Because metals and alloys flow freely when molten, they can be shaped conveniently by casting in an appropriate mold. Casting is particularly useful when very large or complex shapes are to be made—hence the sculptor's use of cast bronze to produce accurate replicas of his work, or the use of casting as the main technique for making ships' propellers, automobile-engine blocks, intricate machine parts, etc. We shall later be discussing casting in detail.

Hot-roll strip. The metal in the upper part of the picture has been rolled hot; from this stage it will be rolled again at a lower temperature, or coiled for shipment.

We have already seen that metals are safe and useful load-bearers because of their ductility. When their elastic limit is reached, they deform plastically rather than shatter. The shaping processes that depend on this plasticity are pressing, rolling, forging, and drawing—known collectively as *working*. Working is divided into two categories, hot and cold working; materials so treated are said to be *wrought*.

The difference between the adjectives *hot* and *cold* here is not arbitrary, as it usually is with these two words; it is precisely governed by the recrystallization temperature of the metal being worked. As we saw, working carried out below this temperature—cold working—creates large numbers of dislocations and other crystal faults, which interfere with one another and with obstructions such as grain boundaries to produce work-hardening. Above the recrystallization temperature, working still produces dislocations and faults, but now the ions move so freely that vacancies and interstitials combine more rapidly than the working process can create them and dislocations are annihilated faster than they are produced. The result is that instead of causing hardening by their mutual interference, the dislocations that are present simply relieve any stresses that might be set up during deformation, and generally make the working process very much easier.

The recrystallization temperature varies from one metal or alloy to another, so that what is a cold-working temperature for one could be a hot-working temperature for another. For instance, pure lead has a recrystallization temperature below normal room temperature. Hence, anything done to lead at normal temperature will be classed as hot working. On the other hand, tungsten is still being cold-worked at over 1000°C, for its recrystallization temperature is 1200°C.

A third way of shaping metals is by cutting, or *machining*. Any material that does not crumble or splinter under the pressure of a cutting tool, but instead forms coherent shavings, can be shaped in this way. With metals this is a finishing process, used only to give the precise shape that is needed, and to add holes, grooves, and so on to blank castings or wrought material. For instance, a component may be made by first casting the basic shape, and then finishing this off by machining out parts that would have been difficult or impossible to incorporate in the initial casting.

Machining is also used to produce small components from stock shapes, such as screws from rods. In this case the process is largely automatic, producing up to several thousands of components an hour.

Again, pieces of metal can be joined together to fabricate relatively complex structures from simpler units. They can be riveted (the equivalent of nailing), bolted (the equivalent of dowelling), glued (a fairly new process using special resins), or welded (in which the metal edges actually melt and fuse together.

Certain metals can be *electroformed*—particularly copper and nickel. The process works on the same principle as electroplating, but in this case the metal is allowed to deposit to a much greater thickness, say half an inch, and the die (or *former*) on which it has been deposited is then removed.

The last main shaping process we should mention is referred to as *powder metallurgy*. Here the metal is first produced as powder, and then made up into the required shapes by placing it in dies and applying both heat and pressure, so that the individual particles stick together.

The powder process is particularly useful for dealing with awkward metals, such as those with very high melting points—like tungsten (3410°C) and platinum (1773·5°C), which are made into blocks from powder and then worked to shape; it is useful, too, for making difficult mixtures such as tungsten and copper, steel and diamond, or bronze and graphite for bearings. Such bearings, into which oil is allowed to soak like water into a sponge, are self-lubricating. They are now quite common in automobiles, washing machines, and other items.

Choosing the Shaping Method

Each of these six basic ways of shaping metals and alloys has its own advantages, and when a designer works on a new product or component he must have all the possibilities clearly in mind. Very often there is overlap, and then the choice of one process in preference to another may depend on a slightly lower cost or on a difference only in the appearance of the finished article. Always the

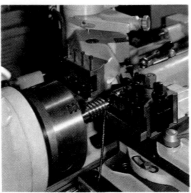

aim must be to produce a component that will be serviceable, but at the lowest overall cost, taking into account not only the cost of material and production, but also, in the case of engineering equipment, the cost of maintenance and replacement when the part is in use.

Apart from other factors, the shaping process may in itself have an important effect on the serviceability of a component. It will, for instance, affect the microstructure, that is, the arrangement of grains, phases, and impurities within the metal, which in turn affects the mechanical properties. Again, cold working or uneven contraction during cooling may introduce stresses into the metal. Those stresses may be aggravated by the stresses the component meets in service, or, if there is close cooperation between designer and metallurgist, they may help to offset their effects. Thirdly, the shaping process will affect the final design of the component, which in turn affects its behavior in service.

The material to be shaped often determines the process to be used, although because there is usually some choice of material the decision may not be rigidly dictated just by this one consideration. If a metal and its alloys are all reasonably ductile, have moderate melting points, and flow well when molten, then, generally speaking, any of the shaping processes can be used. This is true of many copper and aluminum alloys, and to a lesser extent of iron and steel. But in many cases there is a definite restriction that may even go so far as to rule out all processes save one—as, for instance, with metals that have exceptionally high melting points, such as tungsten, which as we saw must usually be shaped in powder form.

Some alloys are brittle at the cold-working temperatures, while others may become brittle in the hot-working range, and in such cases the restriction is obvious. This brittleness is usually due to the presence of a hard second phase, or perhaps to impurities that migrate to grain boundaries as the temperature is raised, causing weakening and hence easy fracture. For instance, the so-called

Opposite: Metal-forming processes and products. Top left: Hot forging. Top right: Cold pressing. Center left: Machining. Center right: Electroformed holes in ·008 in. aluminum strip. Bottom left: Welding. Bottom right: Sintered metal bearings.

cartridge brass is quite ductile when cold, and can easily be deep-drawn into the cartridge cases from which it takes its name.

In the deep-drawing process, which is always carried out cold so as to give stiffness and a good surface finish, a flat sheet of metal (the *blank*) is forced down into a shaped die by a suitable punch. The process is repeated several times, using progressively deeper dies, and the metal must be very ductile to withstand repeated elongation without cracking or tearing. Related to deep drawing are *drawing*, which is just a less drastic version, and *pressing*, which is less drastic still.

But to get back to the cartridge brass: In contrast to its ductility when cold, the alloy becomes brittle and unworkable at high temperatures. Some other brasses, by contrast, are quite brittle when cold, due to the presence of a hard second phase, but are perfectly workable when hot, because the hard second phase dissolves when the temperature is raised a few hundred degrees.

Some processes, such as rolling, can be carried out either hot or cold, so that their use is not ruled out by hot or cold brittleness. But others, such as pressing and drawing, are definitely restricted, in these cases, to cold working. Extrusion, a process in which metal is forced through a shaped hole to form sectioned rods, and forging, in which metal is hammered into shape either with or without the use of a die, must be carried out hot because they involve such great changes in shape or reductions in size that they demand particularly ductile material.

In making castings, whether they be propellers for the Canberra or gold fillings for teeth, it is usually better to use alloys rather than pure metals. A pure molten metal, being uniform, freezes quite sharply at a definite temperature, so that cavities are likely to be formed due to the sudden contraction. Alloys, as we have seen, freeze through a range of temperatures, passing through a mushy stage between being fully liquid and fully solid, in which crystals are mixed with the still-liquid alloy; hence any cavities can be fed by this reservoir of liquid. In general, the wider the gap between the liquidus and solidus, the more suited to casting an alloy will be.

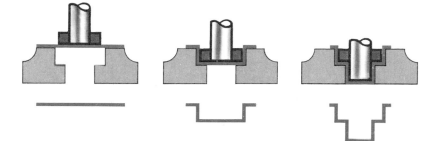

Above: Deep drawing, in three stages.

Right: Cold pressing in split die.

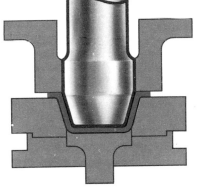

Below: Extrusion of rod.

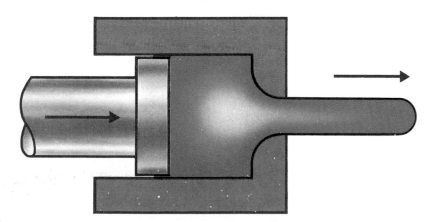

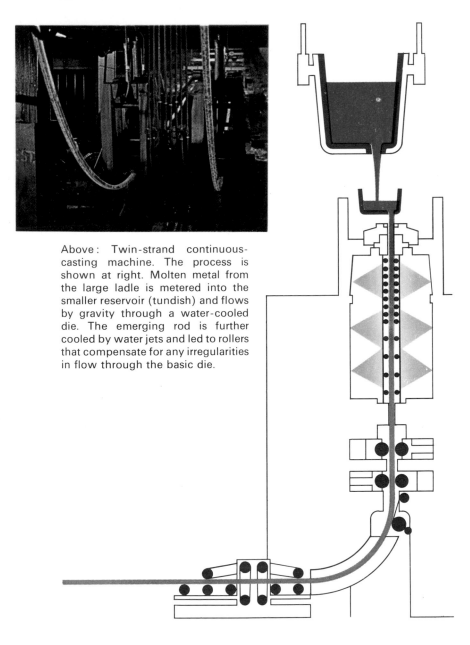

Above: Twin-strand continuous-casting machine. The process is shown at right. Molten metal from the large ladle is metered into the smaller reservoir (tundish) and flows by gravity through a water-cooled die. The emerging rod is further cooled by water jets and led to rollers that compensate for any irregularities in flow through the basic die.

Effects on Microstructure

The effect of various shaping processes on the microstructure of metals and alloys can be very marked, and, as we said above, this in its turn affects the service behavior of the finished component.

Castings generally have coarse grains, with impurities and inclusions randomly distributed. Properties (e.g. tensile strength and ductility) tend to be the same in all directions, but the distribution of impurities produces a relatively low ductility. Castings may also be porous due to the trapping of gases, or because of uneven contraction during solidification.

Although this is true for large and/or slowly cooled castings, such as might be made in sand molds, it is not necessarily true of other types of casting. For instance, die castings, which are produced by injecting relatively small quantities of metal into cold metal dies so that they solidify almost instantly, contain very small grains, and have little or no porosity. Centrifugal castings, usually hollow cylinders such as water main pipes, are made in fast rotating dies that fling the metal outward against the die wall. They have strictly oriented grains that grow inward from the outside, and they are particularly compact and free from porosity. Again, continuous castings, in which molten metal is poured slowly into the top of a metal mold while at the same time the solidified casting is drawn out through a hole in the bottom of the mold, have grains that are elongated along the length of the casting (which may be 40 or 50 feet), while most of the inclusions remain in the molten section for as long as possible and thus tend to gather at one end, which can be cut off. Such a microstructure makes these castings relatively strong in the crosswise direction, and they are more ductile than other castings because they are cleaner. This continuous-casting technique is being used increasingly as a basic production process; with it we can produce long bars and rods more easily than with the traditional hot-rolling of billets. Continuous casting cuts out several stages between the casting of an ingot and the production of the finished material. In contrast to castings in which directional structures are the exception rather than the rule, wrought materials have structures that are inevitably influenced by the direction in which the working has taken place. In general, too, grain sizes are small. In hot-worked material, only

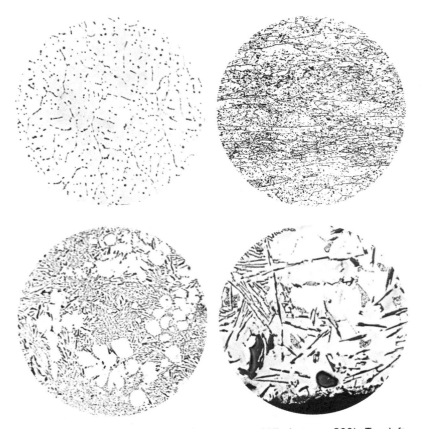

Effects of working methods on microstructure (All photos ×200). Top left: Aluminum ingot as cast. Top right: Same material after cold rolling. Note that grains are reduced in size, and elongated. Below left: Centrifugal casting of aluminum-silicon alloy, section from outer edge. The material here is hard, but tough because of the matrix of almost pure aluminum around the hard brittle aluminum-silicon alloy. Below right: Similar section from inner edge. The slower cooling rate has allowed the dark areas of silicon to separate out, and the material is brittle.

the nonmetallic inclusions are aligned; the metal grains have been continually recrystallizing throughout the working, and hence, although they are small, they are usually nondirectional. As a result, the strength and ductility are generally better in the direction of working. Whether this is beneficial or otherwise depends on the loads the component has to bear. When a metal is cold-worked, its grains become elongated in the direction of working, and they give a similar directionality of properties to that of hot-worked material. Cold working produces hard, strong material, less ductile than hot-worked material. Stresses tend to develop on bends and at narrow sections and if they are allowed to become serious they may lead to failure in service if loads are high.

Influence of Size and Shape on Processing

The size of a component may also have an important influence on the choice of shaping processes. Very large items are best made by sand-casting, by forging, or by joining several smaller units together by welding, brazing, or similar techniques. Small, simply shaped components may be machined from stock such as rod and bar on automatic machines, or if they are more complex and have to be made from material with a relatively low melting point, such as aluminum or zinc or their alloys, then they may be die-cast. Die-casting cannot generally be used for iron and steel and other metals with higher melting points because of the damage they would cause to the steel dies, and dies in more refractory materials would be prohibitively expensive.

Shape, of course, is of prime importance in determining the production process. In general, casting is more suitable for producing complex shapes than are other processes, except perhaps where the component is built up from simple units. In this respect, some casting methods are better than others. Some of the most complicated shapes are made by sand-casting. This involves a great deal of time and money in the preparation of patterns and molds, and there inevitably comes a point when the whole process has to be looked at again to see if a simpler design would not be better.

One of the best methods for producing small or moderately sized castings in small quantities, with very complex shapes and to close tolerances, is investment casting. This process, known to the ancients but lost for centuries, was rediscovered early in the last century by Sir Henry Bessemer, who used it to make replicas of medallions, flowers, and so on. Today it is a vital process in the precision engineering industry. An original, or master pattern, is copied in wax or some other free-flowing, easily melted material, and around this is formed the investment, which is usually some kind of fine, bonded sand sprayed onto the pattern to make an accurately shaped mold. The whole is then placed in an oven,

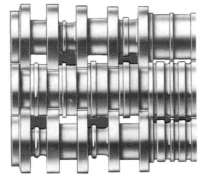

Hot-rolling of bull-head rails. The roll openings shown in color are, from left to right, the sequence through which the rail passes in being shaped. Below: A rail in the final stages of rolling.

where the investment is baked and the wax melted or vaporized, leaving an extremely accurate mold in which the final casting is made. This type of casting involves a great deal of skill, first to keep the accuracy through the various stages of making the master, and then through the copying and recopying; particularly tricky is the problem of making the right allowances for the different expansion and contraction qualities of the metals used.

Accuracy Requirements

The mention of tolerances brings us to the next point, which is that the degree of accuracy needed in a component can be decisive both in choosing the process and in fixing the final cost. Investment casting is, as we said, very accurate—probably the most accurate of processes. Investment-cast components rarely need further treatment; the process can be used for most casting alloys, giving accuracy as fine as a few parts of a thousandth of an inch. Die-casting is also quite accurate, and here again very little finishing is

Below: Upsetting an alloy steel ingot under an 8000-ton electro-hydraulic forging press prior to re-forging it into a rotor shaft.

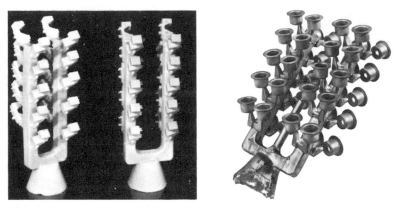

Above: Investment, or lost wax, casting. The model is made in wax, on which the sand mold at far left is made. When the mold is baked, the wax melts and runs out, leaving a cavity into which metal can be cast. At right is a typical final casting.

Below: Casting is the only practical method for making large and complex shapes such as the ship's propeller shown here.

necessary, save for the trimming of surplus material. Cold working can also give close tolerances, again to less than a thousandth of an inch, but hot working is quite bad from this point of view because of scale formation, contraction, and distortion during cooling, while welding and other hot joining processes may also give rise to the formation of a heavy oxide scale and to distortion.

Where we have not achieved high accuracy in the initial shaping of a component, we may have to grind it. Usually the designer has to decide whether the accuracy should be obtained straight away, or a finishing process allowed for; the final answer lies in the nature of the component and the overall costs of the two alternatives. Purpose, material, size, shape, desirable tolerances—these are some of the factors that will decide which shaping method we choose. To them we must add one more: quantity.

The quantity of whatever is to be made is vitally important. Tooling costs in some cases, such as die-casting or drawing, can be very high, so that any components made by these processes should be in large quantities. Also, these processes are easily automated and hence very adaptable to mass production. Sand-casting and investment casting, on the other hand, are best suited to small quantity production and one-off jobs—although even in these cases, of course, repetition helps to spread a little further the cost of pattern making and so on and so reduce total cost.

5 Metals for the Modern World

So far we have been discussing the basic science and technology of metals as it has developed since the middle of the last century. Most of what we have written can be found in the metallurgy textbooks; it serves to set the background against which the rest of the book is to be read. In the chapters that follow we shall be looking at some of the present frontiers of metallurgy—at the current trends in metallurgical thought and technique made necessary by the growth of modern technology. The present chapter will show how metals and alloys are being developed to cope with the increasing stresses and operating temperatures demanded by engineers. Later chapters will discuss some of the new manufacturing techniques, automation, and the latest methods for studying and examining metals and alloys.

Just how far can the process of improvement in the performance of materials go? Are there any fundamental limits; and if so, what are they, and how far have we gone toward reaching them? When we have answered these questions we shall have taken a fair look at

Aluminum oxide (sapphire) whiskers grown in the laboratory ($\times 60$). The larger whiskers will support stresses of 250 tons per square inch, the smaller ones as much as 1500 tons per square inch.

the present state of development of high-strength materials. There is one very obvious limit that we can start with, and that is melting point. The most refractory material we have is carbon, with a melting point of 3500°C. Anything that needs to work above this temperature cannot rely on materials engineering to get it through; it must make use of sophisticated trickery, such as the intense magnetic fields used in fusion research to hold ionized gases at upward of a million degrees. The melting point is a temperature limitation that cannot be avoided. Other limitations, such as softening of the material as the temperature rises toward the melting point and the increase in corrosion rates with temperature, probably can. At least, there is nothing as fundamental as inter-atomic forces to say that these limitations cannot be overcome.

The Strengthening of Metals

As we saw in Chapter 1, there is also the purely mechanical limit of the strength of the ideal crystal. This strength is different for different materials, depending as it does on the particular inter-atomic forces involved. But in all cases this theoretical strength is considerably higher than any strength level that has actually been achieved on a practical scale. The diagram opposite shows the theoretical strength of different materials, and compares it with the highest strength reached in bulk samples, and in fibers, about which we shall have more to say shortly. A glance at this diagram will make it clear that there is plenty of room for improvement.

All conventional techniques for strengthening metals are based on the idea of preventing the movement of dislocations in some way. Alloying, cold working, quenching, aging, and tempering are all ways of doing this.

Precipitation Hardening

The most successful strengthening method yet developed is precipitation hardening, a mechanism discovered just before World War I, as a result of a chance observation during some work then being done on ways of increasing the strength of aluminum alloys for aircraft.

If we take a very ductile metal such as aluminum or copper, we can go quite a long way in hardening it without much danger of

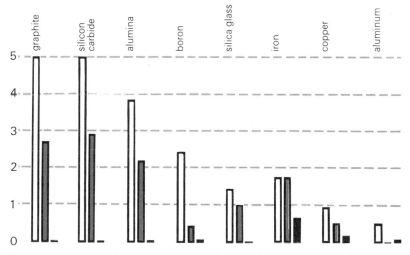

The theoretical and observed strengths of materials. The strengths shown are: the theoretical strength (white), the best strength achieved with fibers of the material (red), and the best strength observed in bulk materials (black).

destroying the crack resistance, by techniques that simply freeze up a proportion of the dislocation movement, such as cold working or ordinary interstitial and substitutional alloying. Nevertheless there is a distinct limit to this, marked by such intermetallic compounds as $CuAl_2$, whose crystal structure is such that all dislocation movement is stopped; but now the material has virtually no resistance to brittle fracture.

Precipitation hardening gets us around this dilemma, and so allows higher strengths to be reached while still retaining a useful amount of ductility. The technique is based on the fact that certain alloy phases soluble at elevated temperatures can, by suitable quenching and tempering procedures, be made to come fully or partially out of solution as a hardening dispersion at around room temperature. The same effect can be got by dispersing particles of hard refractory material in a soft metal matrix—thorium oxide in nickel, for instance—but the technique is less controllable (although more useful at high working temperatures).

In alloys such as this, the hard dispersed particles act as breakers for the long dislocation lines that make the matrix metal ductile. Now there is only local dislocation movement, giving reasonable crack resistance, but combining this with increased strength and increased stiffness. The limiting strength is reached when the stress becomes so high that dislocation lines force their way through the hard particles, or alternatively when the matrix metal begins to rupture around the particles and so form internal fissures. Even so, very large increases in strength can be achieved before there is much danger of this happening, and over the past 50 years precipitation hardening, or age hardening as it is often called, has become far and away the most important alloy-strengthening technique, not only for alloys to be used at room temperatures, but also, as methods have developed, for alloys to be used at very high temperatures, around 1000°c and over.

Probably the most important recent development in precipitation-hardening alloys has been that of the maraging steels. In these steels, which have ultimate strengths of 140–160 tons per square inch, a hardening precipitate is formed in a special carbon-free martensite. In not relying on carbon to give a tough, hard matrix they represent a radical departure from conventional steel-making practice. Carbon has always been regarded as essential to the strength and versatility of iron and steel—economics aside, it was the fact that carbon was an unavoidable impurity in iron that led to the metal's universal success in the first place—but as strengths have been gradually increased over the years, the tendency of carbon to cause brittleness has become more and more troublesome. In the late 1950s the best strength that could be got from alloy steels with normal amounts of carbon and acceptable, although fairly poor, ductility was about 125 tons per square inch. Fairly conventional steels able to carry about 200 tons per square inch *can* be produced, but their ductility and fatigue resistance are so low as to make them practically useless. Clearly carbon had to go. The problem was, how could this be done? All the high-strength steels that had so far been developed relied on the formation of martensite, followed by a precipitation heat treatment, and a toughening process that increased the resilience of the steel without reducing its load-carrying capacity. And martensite had always needed carbon.

Then a team of American metallurgists discovered that if iron containing the minimum possible amount of carbon is alloyed with between 18 and 25 per cent of nickel, it forms a type of martensitic structure, even when slowly cooled. Instead of being hard and brittle, like carbon-based martensite, this new structure was found to be quite tough, and only about half as hard as an untempered carbon martensite. Here was an apparently ideal matrix material for precipitation-hardened high-strength steel. Quite a lot of work was needed to find a suitable alloying recipe to give a good dispersed phase, but eventually variations on the combination of cobalt, molybdenum, titanium, aluminum, and niobium—sometimes leaving out the niobium, at other times the cobalt and molybdenum—were developed. With suitable treatment these allowed the basic nickel-martensite matrix to be strengthened to give tensile strengths of 140 tons per square inch and more, while still being far more resilient than conventional high-strength steels.

These new steels have a number of important attractions apart from their sheer high strength and ductility. For one, the formation of the martensite involves no quenching, and therefore no risk of distortion or cracking as is so often the case with other steels. Also when in the martensitic state the steel is still soft enough to be shaped, cut, bent, and so on quite readily, before the final hardening treatment is applied. And lastly, the hardening treatment itself is now very simple, involving only one heat treatment at a few hundred degrees. Compare this with usual techniques, involving heating for up to several hours at around 900°C, followed by a rapid quench, sometimes to temperatures well below zero, and then the usual tempering to bring out the precipitate.

The production of carbon-free materials, and the large number of expensive alloying additions used, make maraging steels very expensive, and this cost is only partly offset by the cheap processing. Nevertheless, these steels have already found an important place in the space program, and are likely soon to become a valuable addition to the range of high-strength steels available to the modern engineer. Although at first sight they may seem very near to the engineer's dreams, however, maraging steels are not likely to sweep the steel alloy market. There are many common applications for which, technically, they may seem attractive, but economically they are not so.

	Nimonic 75 nickel (1940)	SM-302 cobalt (1960)	SM-322 cobalt (1963)	IN-100 nickel (1963)	M20VC nickel (1964)
hardening elements					
chromium	20%	—	—	10%	10%
titanium	0·3%	—	0·75%	5%	5%
aluminum	—	—	—	5·5%	5·5%
cobalt	—	—	—	15%	10%
refractory elements					
tantalum	—	9%	4·5%	—	—
tungsten	—	10%	9%	—	—
molybdenum	—	—	—	3%	4%
vanadium	—	—	—	0·75%	—
zirconium	—	—	2·25%	—	—

Development of high performance alloys based on nickel or cobalt. The percentage of each alloying constituent is indicated in the body of the table, the basic metal at the top of each column.

Alloys to Work at High Temperatures

When we come to the problem of providing alloys for use at high stresses and high temperatures, for gas-turbine blades and rocket engine parts, as well as for more ordinary applications such as steam-turbine and furnace components, we are faced with the additional problems of general softening of the matrix, as well as with the difficulty of finding a dispersed hardening phase that will remain stable at the operating temperature for as long as the component is required to work at that temperature. The table on page 102 lists some of the typical applications and conditions we are talking about here.

As we said earlier, precipitation hardening depends on the hardening phase being soluble at some elevated temperature; for this reason we have to find an alloy system in which this temperature is well up toward the melting point of the alloy, so that the hardening phase precipitates and is stable at some temperature not far away from this point.

Starting with the Nimonic nickel-chromium alloys, developed at the beginning of the last war for use in Wittle's gas-turbine engines, a whole series of such alloys has in fact been developed, working at ever higher stresses and temperatures. The first of these alloys, Nimonic 75, contained 0·3 per cent titanium and 0·1 per cent carbon, forming a titanium carbide precipitate in the basically 80 : 20 nickel-chromium matrix. Almost immediately an even better alloy was found (containing 2·5 per cent titanium and somewhat less carbon than Nimonic 75), in which the hardening precipitate was an intermetallic compound of nickel and titanium. This alloy, Nimonic 80, was the first of a long series containing titanium, or titanium and aluminum, as hardening agents; in the later ones developed in recent years, a 20 per cent cobalt content has replaced some of the nickel to give a stiffer matrix. Some indication of the advance made since the introduction of the first Nimonic alloys is given by the fact that whereas Nimonic 80 had a specified life of 75 hours at 38,000 pounds per square inch and 700°C, one of the more recent alloys in the series, Nimonic 115, is designed to meet a specification of 75 hours' life at 14,000 pounds per square inch and 980°C; at this temperature Nimonic 80 would be able to bear less than 2000 pounds per square inch for the 75 hours. With the coming of the Space Age, further development of the heat-resisting alloys based on various combinations of nickel, chromium, and cobalt, with a variety of hardening additions, has become increasingly important. Such alloys, known generally as " Superalloys," are vital to the development of rocket engines working at ever higher temperatures, as well as to a great deal of more earthy equipment. All form stable oxide films at around

700°C, giving good corrosion protection at service temperatures that now may be around 1100°C. There are two main groups of Superalloys—those based on nickel, and those based on cobalt. The trend in both groups has been to increase the content of hardening elements well beyond the levels found in the Nimonic heat-resisting alloys. Use has also been made of additions of refractory metals such as tantalum, tungsten, niobium, and molybdenum, all of which have melting points well above 2400°C, and of several metals with melting points in the 1800–2200°C range. Such high-melting additions are all designed to give highly stable hardening precipitates. The table on page 102 illustrates this trend.

In spite of these developments, which have led to the use of solution temperatures near to the melting point of the alloys, and even to alloys that precipitate on cooling directly from the liquid state, and thus have to be cast in shape, the strengths achieved at temperatures above 700–800°C amount to only a few tons per square inch; even 10 tons per square inch would be regarded as exceptionally strong at around 1000°C. This is far from satisfactory, especially when we remember that theoretically a crystalline structure should retain its strength right up to its melting point, provided that it develops no defects. Techniques in which refractory oxides are dispersed inside metals—nickel hardened by thorium oxide, for instance—have given some improvement, but still far from enough. Using this method, strengths of around 1/1000th of Young's modulus, at 0·7 of the melting point measured on the Kelvin or absolute scale, have been reached. Young's modulus, E, is a figure that measures the stiffness of a material at room temperature.

In practical terms, if a metal could be subjected to a load equivalent to its Young's modulus (which is expressed in pounds or tons per square inch), its length would double. In fact, of course, were it not exceptionally ductile, the metal would fracture long before this amount of strain was reached. For a steel, a strength of 1/1000th of E at 0·7 of the melting point would be 13–14 tons per square inch at about 1100°C, which is still less than one tenth of the best performances at room temperature, which are themselves far from the possible limits.

Fiber Reinforcement

Clearly, conventional strengthening techniques are at full stretch, and yet they are nowhere near doing justice to the potentialities of crystalline materials. An entirely new approach is needed.

In the last few years this required new approach has been provided by the technique of reinforcing metals with fibers. In this, the idea is not so much to interfere directly with the motion of dislocation in the matrix, but rather to use the flow of the stressed matrix to transfer load to bundles of strong fibers embedded in it. The strength of the composite then depends very much upon the strength of the fibers and the efficiency with which the load is transferred to them; this is in marked contrast to conventional precipitation-hardened materials, in which the bulk of the load is still taken by the matrix, and whose strength never comes anywhere near the strength of the precipitates.

Why fibers? Well, first of all, because they can be made exceptionally strong. The table on page 99 lists some typical tensile strengths of fibers and fiber-shaped materials, together with the strengths of some ordinary engineering materials. Let us look at some of the reasons for this high strength of fibers.

At the beginning of this chapter we discussed the two principal mechanisms by which materials are weakened, namely, the movement of dislocations, and the propagation of cracks. We saw how, in general, as the importance of one decreases in a material, so the importance of the other increases—as the material becomes stronger through the locking-up, or the absence, of dislocations, so it becomes more crack-prone, and vice versa. For various reasons that depend on the type of material involved, many fibers manage to avoid these difficulties, at least to a certain extent.

Take, for instance, the case of the so-called metal " whiskers." These are minute single crystals, shaped literally like whiskers, that can be grown in a number of ways—by electrolysis, by vapor condensation, during certain kinds of chemical reaction, and so on. They are only a few microns thick, and rarely more than a few millimeters long.

Metallurgists and physicists have been interested in these tiny fiber-like crystals for several years now, ever since it was discovered

Iron whiskers, virtually perfect crystals ($\times 11$).

that their strength was often very near to, or even sometimes as high as, the theoretical strength calculated for a perfect single crystal. They have become an important subject of study, both from the viewpoint of fundamental crystal physics, and because of what they might teach us about the problem of making high-strength materials.

The strength of metal whiskers depends critically upon their diameter, increasing as the diameter is reduced, and rising sharply below a diameter of 10 μm. At this size the crystals are near perfect, with no dislocations and no significant surface defects. Stress-strain curves produced for such whiskers show them to have a remarkably large range of elastic deformation, sometimes as high as 4 or 5 per cent. Most commercial engineering materials fail at a working elastic strain of around 0·1 per cent. After this there is usually a sudden yielding, followed by immediate fracture, or a great deal of rapid plastic flow. Unfortunately this high-strength state of ductile metal whiskers does not last very long. Dislocations soon appear, perhaps as a result of surface oxidation or some other surface action, and the whisker weakens rapidly. Thus, from a practical point of view, metal whiskers as such are at present

Progress of cracks in a bundle of fibers, each of which is assumed to be a virtually perfect crystal. Lateral cracks have little effect on longitudinal strength, being stopped by fiber boundaries.

useless, even assuming that we can get over the problems of growing and harvesting them economically in useful quantities. However, ductile metals are not the only materials that can be produced as whiskers or ultrafine fibers. Most materials can be produced in this form, and what is more, many of them do not suffer from weakness caused by dislocations.

Materials such as brittle metals or crystalline nonmetals can thus give us very strong fibers that will not soften; but now they are exceedingly crack-prone, and it would seem that we are back where we started. However, this is only so if we consider individual fibers. If we consider bundles of parallel fibers we get a somewhat different situation. Fibers of ductile metals, it is true, will still weaken fairly quickly as dislocations form, and this will happen throughout the bundle, giving the same result as with a single fiber. Brittle fibers, on the other hand, retain their strength until cracks begin to form, as with the material in bulk, but now, by using bundles of fibers, we have provided effective barriers to the spread of cracking—a crack in an individual fiber cannot spread across the whole bundle because of the interfaces between the fibers, and thus the disastrous effects of transverse cracking should be greatly reduced. The diagram on page 107 shows how longitudinal cracks travel harmlessly along the fiber lengths.

Be this as it may, a bundle of fibers a few millimeters long at the most is not an engineering material. We must provide some way of holding the fibers together, of transferring applied load to them, and also protecting their surfaces to reduce still further the damage caused by surface imperfections leading to cracking. A useful clue is provided by the example of glass fibers. In that case fibers of a classically brittle amorphous substance, glass, are bonded together with a resin to make a tough, crack-proof, lightweight composite. The functions of the resin are, first, to hold the fibers together; secondly, to contain any cracks that develop in the fibers, and so render them harmless; and thirdly, to act as a means of transferring the applied load to the fibers. Thus, if we replace the resin by a ductile metal and the glass by stronger, brittle fibers, we shall have something like the material we are aiming at. The point about load transfer is fundamental to the whole philosophy behind the use of fibers, instead of some other form, for reinforcement. It might be argued that the particles of precipitate in an ordinary age-hardening material, even when relatively coarse by age-hardening standards, are still fine enough to possess ideal strength, and hence if we can introduce enough of them—filling, say, half the volume of the material—then we shall get a great increase in strength simply from their direct load-bearing capacity. According to this we should not need fibers at all; just more precipitate, or a dense dispersion of a stable oxide.

The trouble with this argument is that it does not take account of the difficulties of load transfer from the matrix to the particles. The problem is rather like the difference between gripping a small ball or a piece of string. A spherical or near-spherical object of this size does not provide enough area for grip, so that long before the stress has reached even comparatively moderate levels, by the standards with which we are now dealing, the matrix begins to pull away from each particle. In other words, over the short distances involved, spherical particles do not strain enough to follow the larger strains of the matrix. With a fiber oriented in the direction of the load, this problem does not arise, for, provided the aspect ratio of the fiber is above a certain minimum, its central position will strain at

Function of ductile matrix in transferring load evenly to strong but brittle fiber.

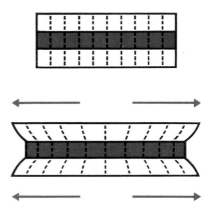

the same rate as the matrix—which can take grip—and so the load is transferred smoothly. Even when the matrix begins to flow plastically the load is transferred in this way, and the composite should deform elastically right up to its breaking point. Also, theoretically, with a fiber that does not soften, we should be able to get high strengths right up to the melting point of the matrix.

These, then, are the principles behind the development of fiber-reinforced metals. Having extolled the virtues of these materials, it remains for us to take a look at some of their possible disadvantages, and finally to look at some of the systems that might be developed.

Many difficulties liable to be associated with fiber-reinforced metals arise directly from the combination of two different types of material, and from the unique microstructure involved. During cyclic loading, for instance, stress concentrations at the fiber ends may lead to some extension of cracking into the matrix. Also, because the matrix is taking repeated excursions into and out of the plastic range, it may exhibit rather poor fatigue resistance. Wear resistance, too, might be poor, because of the very abrasive nature of any debris produced. And finally, of course, there is the trouble caused by the very different coefficients of thermal expansion of metal and fibers (unless, as is possible, the fibers are also metal). All these snags are being investigated as materials are developed. More important at this stage, however, are the difficulties that arise out of the peculiar manufacturing needs—fibers have to be grown and harvested, incorporated in the metal and correctly aligned according to the designed stress distribution, and then the composite has to be processed, and probably joined. The remainder of this chapter will be spent discussing some of the fiber-metal composites at present under development, and we shall see how some of these difficulties are being resolved.

First let us look at some of the work that is being done on reinforcement with metal fibers, which is about as close to conventional metallurgy as we can come in this field. Here the idea is to use fibers of the more refractory metals such as molybdenum, tantalum, and tungsten, relying on the matrix to protect them from the rapid oxidation to which they are prone at high temperatures.

One such set of composites, developed by an American team, consists of 0·005 in. diameter cold-worked molybdenum fibers in pure titanium and titanium alloyed with 6 per cent aluminum and 4 per cent vanadium. Both these materials, when unreinforced, maintain good strength-to-weight ratios up to 500°C; the introduction of fibers aimed to raise this temperature. To make the composites (containing 10, 20, 30, and 40 per cent fiber), molybdenum wires (which can be produced at this small diameter by ordinary cold drawing) were cut to 0·1–0·25 in. lengths and blended with powdered titanium or titanium alloy, then the whole thing cold-pressed and sintered, and finally extruded and cold-rolled to rod. Apart from producing the composite in a convenient form for testing, these last processes had the effect of aligning the fibers, and of extending them to about 6 inches in length and 0·002 inches in diameter.

Results of tensile strength tests with these rods are impressive. The addition of 20 per cent molybdenum fibers to pure titanium results in a 100 per cent improvement at a temperature of 200°C, while rods made from the heavily reinforced (40 per cent) titanium-aluminum-vanadium alloy retain their 75 per cent improvement in strength very well at temperatures in the region of 540°C. Unfortunately, no ductility figures are available for these composites; but apparently they were quite good. Trouble arose because the oxidation of molybdenum was not completely prevented by the matrix, while there was found to be a definite limit

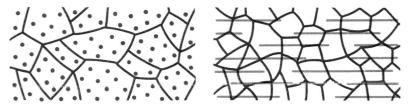

Reinforcing effect in precipitation-hardened materials (left), and fiber-reinforced materials (right). Clearly the ductile matrix grips the fibers better than the roughly spherical grains of precipitate.

on the upper working temperature because of the tendency of the molybdenum and titanium to dissolve in one another, thus gradually canceling the fiber effect.

Also in the United States, at the Clevite Corporation, work goes on to develop metal-metal composites using Nichrome (a heat-resisting alloy based on nickel and chromium), cobalt, cobalt alloy 605, and stainless steel as matrices. These are all traditionally heat-resisting materials, and so make obvious starting points. Tungsten fibers are used for reinforcement, and, as with the molybdenum-titanium composites, mixing and fabrication are done by powder metallurgical techniques.

Instead of aligning short fibers along the direction of stress, the Clevite experiments compared the results from a number of different arrangements—namely, unreinforced, reinforced with continuous wires, with discontinuous aligned fibers, with discontinuous random fibers, and with continuous wires arranged as a " mat " with alternate layers at right angles.

Surprisingly, some fibers were found actually to weaken the matrix at room temperature, but to have a distinct strengthening effect at 1100°C. This happened with tungsten-stainless steel, and tungsten-Nichrome composites, and was probably due either to interpenetration of tungsten with the nickel, chromium, or iron, or to the formation at the interface of some intermetallic compound brittle at room temperature. When the tungsten was plated with cobalt the trouble disappeared. Recrystallization and oxidation are also held effectively in check by this cobalt layer, which thus has a double effect in enhancing the fiber strengthening.

In the cobalt-tungsten system the intermetallic bond was not strong enough, and fibers tended to be pulled out; once again a layer of cobalt provided a cure, as did surface activation with palladium chloride, and the formation of tungsten carbide at the interface of the fiber and the matrix.

Most of the composites so far tested at Clevite have shown strengths approaching 90 per cent of the theoretical. In some cases, however, strengths at 1100°C were greater than predicted, probably because interdiffusion gave some solid solution strengthening.

One metal that seems particularly suited to use as a reinforcing fiber in the production of high strength-to-weight ratios is beryllium, which itself has a high strength-to-weight ratio, as well as being quite stiff. So far, however, attempts to incorporate beryllium fibers in experimental composites with matrixes of silver and of a silver-aluminum-germanium alloy have failed. The thinnest fibers broke up during compacting and tended to coalesce into spheroids. Bonding of other fibers was poor, and the overall result was that the composites were not even as strong as others made by using beryllium powder instead of fibers. The general run of beryllium fibers will have to be improved before there is any hope of making successful composites from them.

The possibility of reinforcing metals with various kinds of whiskers, which, as we saw, are fibers grown as single crystals, has probably been the subject of more speculation and experiment than any of the other systems. At the same time it is furthest away from realization. The main difficulty lies in growing, harvesting, and aligning the whiskers, and quite a lot of the experimental work so far done has been on these problems. However, a number of actual composites are being studied, mostly as models to give an insight into the fundamentals of their behavior rather than as practical systems. One of the most important of these studies is that being made on sapphire whiskers (aluminum oxide) in silver, at the Missiles and Space Division of the General Electric Corporation, as a preliminary step toward the production of a material five times as strong as the best Superalloys at 1100°C.

At first the sapphire whiskers for these composites were produced by passing an oxidizing gas over a bath of molten aluminum held in a furnace at 1500°C, which is well over twice the melting point of the aluminum. This produced an aluminum oxide (alumina) vapor, which condensed as whiskers on the sides of the bath. By adjusting the temperature, and the dew point and flow rate of the gas, the quality of the whiskers could be controlled. Unfortunately, the necessary conditions varied from batch to batch, while the production rate was only 1 gram per week. Hence a continuous method was devised in which a molybdenum collecting base moves relative to the source of the alumina vapor.

Once the whiskers have been collected they are sorted and the best ones chosen to go into composites. This is a slow method—it would be quicker just to use all the whiskers in the form of a wool—and it restricts the choice of matrix to those metals with good flow properties, but it probably gives the best control for fundamental experiments of this kind. The individual whiskers are cleaned, either chemically or by an ion bombardment technique, and then coated with a thin layer of platinum, whose function is to protect the crystal surface during the manufacture of composites, and to help in forming a strong bond with the matrix. The treated whiskers are then packed in a mold, particular care being taken to avoid getting a preponderance of fiber ends in one place.

So far tests on these composites have shown that the manufacturing difficulties have not been overcome, and ideal bonding has not yet been achieved. Whiskers were often seen protruding from the fracture face, suggesting that the bond had been too weak to transfer sufficient load to the fibers to break them. Even so, quite good strengths have been measured, although according to theoretical calculations only about 54 per cent of the reinforcing potential has so far been achieved.

Silver provides a good matrix for model experiments of this kind, but if actual service temperatures of 1100°C are to be aimed at, much more refractory matrixes, such as nickel, steel, platinum, and palladium, will have to be used. Since 1960, work on alumina reinforcement of nickel-base and iron-base alloys has been going on at the laboratories of Horizons Inc., sponsored by the U.S. Bureau of Naval Weapons, with a view to finding new materials for use in missiles, spacecraft, and aircraft.

The whiskers used in this case are grown in much the same way as at G.E.C., but the method of making the composites is quite different. Once separated from each other, the whiskers are dispersed in water, together with a powder form of the matrix metal, and a wetting agent. When thoroughly mixed the dispersion is filtered, the mass broken up and mixed with a small amount of methyl cellulose binder and water, then extruded to align the whiskers. The resulting " green " rods are dried, sintered, and then cold-rolled.

So far, with whisker contents up to 20 per cent, strengths of around 120,000 lb. per square inch at room temperature, and 75,000 lb. per square inch at 480°C, have been achieved. These are around 70 per cent of what theory says is possible, and show that alumina reinforcement of Nichrome and iron-base alloys is at least feasible. In one isolated case, a composite with a 36 per cent fiber content was tested to 237,000 lb. per square inch—a reinforcement of 280 per cent. Other work on whisker reinforcement of this kind is going on, but so far none of it has reported results as successful as these. The main troubles have come from finding a way of making good-quality whiskers, and getting them to bond well with the matrix; it seems likely to be some time before anything approaching a commercial material is produced.

Meanwhile, other research lines are pushed ahead. Apart from the metal wires we talked about earlier, the only other fibers available in quantity are those made by conventional glass-drawing processes. For these to be applied successfully to a material it must be viscous over a wide temperature range, and the only ones that really fill this bill are silica and silicate-base glasses, which are not much stiffer than ordinary aluminum. Even so, they can be, and are being, used to give some reinforcement, while efforts are being made to produce stiffer glasses that can be drawn.

The fact that glass will not withstand high temperatures is another limitation. Silicate glasses tend to lose their strength at 300°C, although silica is a little better. Even so, using these fibers, the range of temperatures over which aluminum and magnesium can be used can be extended to well above that possible by conventional techniques. The Owens-Corning Fiberglas Corporation, for instance, have produced a glass-reinforced aluminum alloy that gives a strength of 30,000 lb. per square inch up to 350°C, while at Rolls Royce an aluminum-silica composite has been produced that gives strengths of over 50,000 lb. per square inch, although these

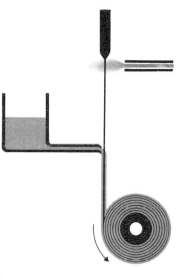

Reinforcement of aluminum rod with silica. The molten aluminum is condensed around the hot silica thread.

tend to fall off rather rapidly above 200°C (but even then the material is stronger than other aluminum alloys). The diagram on this page shows how the fibers for this composite are made. No further aluminum is added, the thin coating from the feed tube acting as a protective coating and as the matrix metal.

Graphite is another material that might well be used for reinforcement; it is three times as stiff as steel, and retains this stiffness to over 2000°C. But so far no successful method for growing whiskers has been developed.

Although the bulk of the development work on fiber-reinforced metals is concentrated on fundamental investigations and tentative experiment, we can round off the chapter with a few practical composites that have been developed. For instance, in the United States there is an aluminum-glass composite in which the glass is dosed with nuclear fuel, giving a crack-free fuel element for small reactors. Lead reinforced with bronze or steel is being used for bearings and for strong soldering tape. The most important thing here, though, is the ability of the fibers to retain molten lead by capillary action—to stop too rapid disintegration of the bearing when overheated, or to allow better control of soldering.

The good thermal properties of copper can now be taken advantage of at higher temperatures by using a copper-tungsten composite—this being used in rocket nozzles—while a silver-steel composite is being used to make seals for aircraft fuel systems operating between 50°C and 650°C.

6 New Ways of Fabricating Metals

There are many areas of modern production where the return on improvements in conventional assembly techniques—increased automation, for instance—is reaching a level such that further progress in this direction is scarcely worthwhile under current economic conditions. There is no point in producing things faster if you cannot also sell them faster. At the same time new technologies are demanding the use of new materials, many of them difficult to handle, as well as more complex shapes. And at all times industrial economics demand that processes be made cheaper and still cheaper. All these pressures have combined in the last year or two to stimulate the development of a range of new techniques for the fabrication of metals, capable of giving great reductions in production time, making more efficient use of the available material—reducing waste from 60 or even 90 per cent to 10 per cent or less—and allowing the economic production of shapes so complex that hitherto they would have been prohibitively expensive. This is on top of the many important advances in basic metal production

Explosive forming under water. In one process, the explosion forms hemispherical domes (visible in background) from aluminum blanks 14 feet in diameter.

—oxygen steel-making, continuous casting, vacuum refining, and so on—that in the last few years have combined to hold down the steadily rising costs of producing basic metals and alloys.

The aim of any metal-shaping process should be to produce the required component in as few separate operations as possible, in the shortest time, and with the least waste; the absolutely ideal version of this would be a process that could produce a component from a single cold billet in one operation, taking no time, and with so perfect a shape that it needed no aftertreatment whatsoever.

Nearest to this ideal are the various forging, stamping, pressing, and extrusion techniques already available, and it is from these that some of the most important newer methods have been developed. Advanced cutting, machining, and joining techniques are also being evolved, and we shall discuss these later in the chapter. But first let us look at some of the methods by which components are produced by direct shaping.

Shaping Under Pressure

It is almost 70 years since the discovery that the reduction in area of a tensile test bar at fracture is much greater when the testpiece is surrounded by a superimposed hydrostatic pressure than when it is not. Just why there should be this increase in effective ductility is still not completely clear, but two reasons are usually given. One is that the pressure prevents voids spreading from points of internal weakness that might otherwise act as initial sources of fracture. The second is that fracture does occur, but the pressure almost immediately welds the two sides together again.

Until recently there has been no point in exploiting this property of metals, simply because it was unlikely that any method devised would be substantially better than conventional hot forging or hot extrusion to make it worth the trouble. In recent years, however, more " difficult " metals have come into use, particularly in aviation and space applications, whose ductility is so low that they cannot stand much deformation before they crack, even at quite high fabrication temperatures. This applies not only to high-strength steels and alloys of refractory metals, but also to many of the modern aluminum alloys. Because of this the possibility of fabricating these materials under high hydrostatic pressure is being

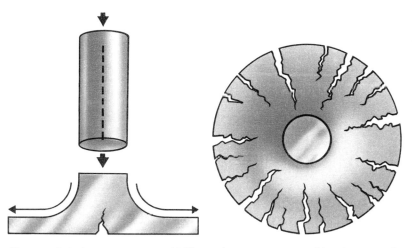

Characteristic fracture pattern of billet under ram pressure without surrounding counter pressure.

taken more seriously; development projects are under way, and some are now approaching the point of practical application.

Typical, in principle at least, of all the methods being looked at is that developed at the Thompson Engineering Laboratory of the General Electric Company in the United States. The general setup for a forging rig is shown on page 120. This consists of a split-die, at the center of which is a cavity the shape of the part to be made, with a vertical access-bore for the metal billet and a ram. Before forging starts the cavity is filled with a matrix material that flows viscously and can transfer pressure hydrostatically like a fluid. Several such materials were tried out, to find one that combined the required viscosity and hydrostatic characteristics with reasonable lubricating power; the one finally chosen was Cerrobend, a low-melting alloy of 50 per cent bismuth, 26·7 per cent lead, 13·3 per cent tin, and 10·0 per cent cadmium.

When the billet is driven into the cavity by the ram the pressure in there naturally rises, as the matrix has nowhere to go; eventually it rises to such a level that it forces apart the two halves of the die. The matrix can then flow outward and the highly compressed metal flows into the cavity. There is clearly a danger here that the

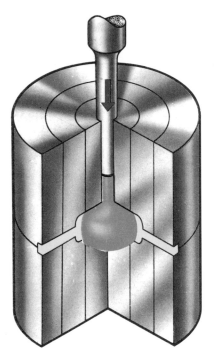

Split-die forging rig using force-fitted (i.e. prestressed) concentric rings to contain forming pressure. The fluid furnishing the counter pressure is metered from the die via the yellow channels, maintaining the required counter pressure.

high pressure will cause the die material to deform as well as the billet. The General Electric engineers have got around this by arranging to build a compressive stress, acting inward, into the die, against which the outward-pushing tensile stress of the forging operation can work. They do this by making up the die from force-fitted concentric rings, each one pressing in on the ones inside it, so that the inner ring, which is of tungsten carbide with a compressive strength of 540,000 lb. per square inch, is prestressed to 450,000 lb. per square inch. This means that the cavity pressure must reach this level before the die will even begin to deform.

Tests on aluminium alloys at 20,000–30,000 lb. per square inch back pressure have been successful in producing crack-free forgings at deformation ratios of up to 19 : 1, but so far the technique has not given good surface finish or accuracy. Neither has the equipment yet been made to operate smoothly. Similar troubles have been met in other hydrostatic fabrication techniques, most of which involve extrusion rather than upset forging, and most of which use a liquid instead of a viscous fluid.

Shaping at Ultrahigh Speed

More successful in practice, although when looked at coldly less spectacularly promising, has been high-energy-rate forming, of which explosive forming is just one of the better-known examples. Whereas hydrostatic forming is still in the development stage, high energy-rate forming is now an accepted production technique, for conventional and new metals, for mass production, and for large or intricate one-off jobs.

When this method of production was first seriously discussed (it had been thought about in the last century, but has only become a real possibility in the last two decades) the claims for it were very enthusiastic. Some of the first modern experiments had shown that if the rate of deformation of a metal was greatly increased, its ductility seemed to increase in a way very similar to the increase caused by high hydrostatic pressure. Here was a technique that would lead to the complete replacement of all existing fabrication techniques. But this early enthusiasm was ill-founded; later, more careful work has not confirmed the first conclusions, which were probably based on misinterpretation of the evidence, and in fact no good model of metal behavior at high strain rates has yet been developed. Nevertheless the ball had been set rolling, and there began an intensive program of investigation into the characteristics and patterns of behavior of metals at high strain rates, to see if there really was a new technique available, even though it might not be as revolutionary as had at first been thought. The result has been the introduction of several methods for high-energy-rate formation, each with its own particular advantages, which, while not replacing the old techniques, have added to the range of things that can be done to shape metals.

High-energy-rate forming pushes energy into a workpiece at a very high rate, and ultimately, of course, it is the energy we apply that is important. The kinetic energy of a body—a moving hammer, for instance—is more sensitive to a change in velocity than to a change in mass. (This follows easily from the $E = \frac{1}{2}mv^2$ relationship.) Thus the effect of increasing tool velocity can be to give a much higher energy input for the same tool mass, or the same energy input for a much smaller tool mass, or to increase the energy input while still allowing some reduction in tool mass.

What is really important in deciding the effect of increased tool velocity in fabrication is the toughness of the metal we are dealing with—that is, its ability to absorb energy without fracturing. The tougher a metal, the more work we can put into it before it begins to break up. (We can deform a ductile metal a great deal, but the amount of energy we put into it before it is so thin that it starts to crack may not be very much compared with the amount of energy a high-strength steel might absorb.) If we measure the toughness of metals at various strain rates we find that in every case there is an optimum strain rate, above which the toughness begins to fall off. Clearly it is not worth deforming a metal at a rate faster than this optimum. Thus for any process we have to know the optimum strain rate of the metal, from which we can calculate the maximum rate at which we can safely push energy into the workpiece. Both involve complex calculations and estimations that need not bother us here.

So far, five main sources of high-speed energy have been used to fabricate metals. These are chemical explosives, electrostatic discharge, magnetic fields, pneumatic-mechanical devices, and ultrasonic devices. Of the five, chemical explosives have so far been the most widely exploited, but all the others show great promise.

Explosive Forming

A very wide range of metals has already been successfully shaped using explosives, including aluminum and its alloys, stainless steel, magnesium and its alloys with aluminum and with thorium, titanium and its alloys with aluminum and with vanadium and manganese, copper and its alloys, and the refractory metals molybdenum, tantalum, tungsten, and niobium. Almost any shape can be formed at almost any size, without the need for machinery, with a simple, light die and no foundations other than a fairly massive base to absorb the shock. The great advantage of explosive forming over other methods, however, lies in its ability to produce large or very complex shapes to tolerances as close as 0·002 in., with little or no need for aftermachining. Thus, although it is essentially a one-off process, it can be cheap because of the great savings in capital costs, tooling, etc. Even the dies can be cheap, being made of such substances as epoxy resin, concrete, and so on.

Both high and low explosives are used, the choice depending on the shape being made, and on whether the charge is in direct contact with the blank, or, as is more usual, a standoff technique is used.

In the latter the explosive charge is fired some distance away from the workpiece and die, the shock being transmitted to them as a wave through a transmitting fluid, usually water. In this way a much more even spread of the deforming force is achieved, allowing the use of more powerful explosives. The setup is shown in the diagram on page 124. It is best for shaping sheet, plate, and tubes, and for sizing and flanging, while close-contact operations are used for extrusion, cladding, compacting, and bonding of metal powders, and for surface hardening of such materials as Hadfield manganese steel and stainless steels.

Standoff forming with explosives (see diagrams on page 124) is usually done either in a water-filled tank sunk in the ground, or in a tank in which the water (or any other suitable transmitting fluid) is contained in a bag made from some disposable material such as polythene. The first method is used for large components requiring large charges, where the water serves not only as a transmitter but also to deaden the noise and as a safety device, in that it absorbs the explosion. For full deformation the space between the blank and the die is sealed off and evacuated. For lighter parts where a deeper draw is needed, the technique of free-forming is used, for which there is no die, the metal simply deforming into the open space below it. The success of this depends on the achievement of a uniform shock wave, to give even deformation. Developed from this is the plug-cushion technique, in which the effect of the shock wave on the blank is controlled by the cushioning of selected areas, thus allowing more overall deformation than would otherwise be possible.

The two possible setups for forming complex cylinders are shown on page 125. The closed system, in which low explosives are used, is designed for making small cylindrical components, in which there is not enough standoff distance for the use of high explosives. By closing the ends of the cylinder in this case the light blast is concentrated and the shock wave maintained for a period long enough to allow adequate deformation. Where high explosives can be used, the cylinder ends must be kept open (and hence a

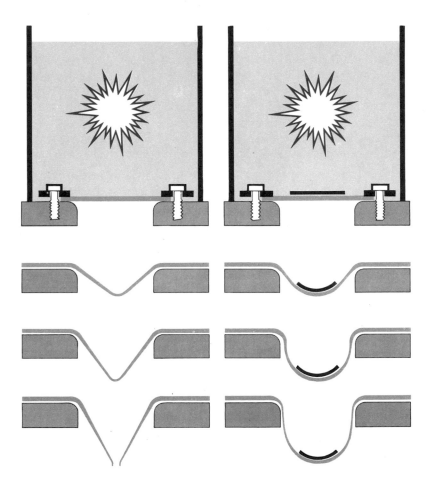

Above: Explosive forming, using a liquid to transmit force. In the left-hand diagram the liquid presses directly on the metal, giving the shape shown, with weakness at the tip. Use of the plug (right) gives a more uniform deformation with the thinning distributed around the walls.

Opposite: Low- and high-pressure cylindrical forming. The low-pressure method (left) is used for thin-wall cylinder forming and the liquid is contained in a sealed chamber. In the high-pressure process, used for forming thicker-wall cylinders, the more concentrated explosion required makes it impossible to seal the chamber.

polythene bag used to contain the transmission fluid) to moderate the very high peak pressure.

With large deformations or very complex shapes one firing will probably be insufficient, in which case, of course, several will have to be used; but this is simply a matter of replacing the charge as many times as necessary, without disturbing the die setup.

Close-contact explosive-forming operations are particularly useful in cladding or welding where dissimilar metals are to be joined by a diffusion bond. The diagram on page 126 gives a general idea of how this is done. The two surfaces to be joined are placed together with a slight angle between them, and wrapped around the sheet of explosive separated from the metal surfaces with some layer that protects their finish. When the explosive is fired at the line of contact of the plates, passing simultaneously up each side, it forces them together, squeezing out a jet of molten metal, which serves as a fusing medium.

Some work on extrusion and forging has been done, in which the explosive is used to accentuate the action of a mechanical ram. The great attraction here lies in the possibility of working more difficult metals, since there is little time for the tools to get overheated because the action is so rapid. At the same time, because the metals being shaped behave rather differently at these high strain rates than they do at the rates of conventional extrusion and forging, it has been found that there is considerably less die wear. In one case

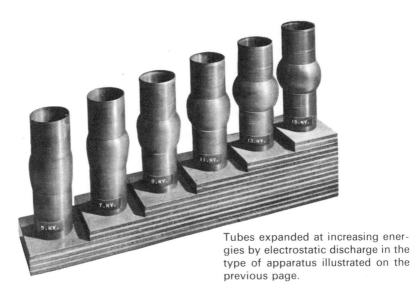

Tubes expanded at increasing energies by electrostatic discharge in the type of apparatus illustrated on the previous page.

tungsten billets were extruded at 1900°C, being reduced to 1/40th of their original diameter in one pass through the die—which was of a very ordinary tool steel—yet the dies stood up to several such shots without any appreciable wear.

The most promising field of contact explosive operations, however, lies in the compacting, shaping, and bonding of powdered metals. These materials are becoming increasingly important in fabrication metallurgy, particularly for forming complex shapes from difficult metals, or from metal and metal-ceramic mixtures that could not be made and formed any other way; they are also important where the porosity or density of the component needs to

Explosive forming used to make bimetal laminates. Sheet explosive fired against one face throws the metal sheets together, causing them to weld at the interface.

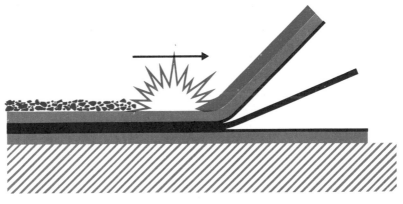

be carefully controlled. (The most widespread use of such materials is probably in the numerous self-lubricating bearings that we now find in our everyday lives, in which the oil has been absorbed and is held by capillary action in the fine pores of a powdered-metal compact.) The advantage of explosive compacting lies not only in its speed, but also in the uniformity of compacting and the very high compact densities that can be achieved—sometimes as high as 96 per cent of the theoretical density of the metal, which is much higher than is achieved by many other methods, including casting and forging. Apart from compacting, which is just the initial stage of any powder-fabrication process, bonding and shaping can be carried out in an explosive-operated press with double acting pistons. (Bonding is an essential stage in any powder-metallurgical process, in which the individual particles are actually welded together, either by heating the compact under pressure, or by fusion welding brought about by very high pressures alone.)

Finally, contact explosive forming using sheet explosives is used to harden the surface of Hadfield steels (whose surface transforms to martensite on heavy impact) and stainless steels, where the hardening is simply caused by the intense cold working. The usual method for doing this, in which steel shot is fired at the surfaces (*shot peening*) gives a thin hard shell about 0·05 in. thick, which ends suddenly at that depth. Explosive hardening gives a shell up to 2 in. thick, whose hardness falls off gradually toward the interior of the component. One of the most important uses of the technique so far has been in the in situ hardening of Hadfield manganese steel railroad points, and of the working edges of mining equipment.

Explosive forming techniques used for powder-metal compacting. In this method a pair of free pistons are fired against the side of a compact.

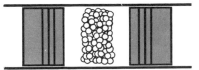
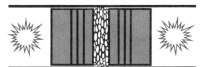

Hydroelectric Forming

Most of the other high-energy-rate forming processes are still in the development stage rather than in use as regular production techniques, but we must give them a brief mention, for it is clear that they will all eventually become important in their own right.

In hydroelectric forming a shock wave rather like that from a chemical explosion is formed under water by a heavy spark discharge from a bank of condensers, or by the very rapid vaporization of a wire connecting the sparking electrodes. In the first case the spark produces a plasma that expands rapidly as a gas bubble, transmitting the energy of the spark to the workpiece. In the second case the wire vaporizes to something like 25,000 times its original volume, and again produces a plasma shock wave. Using aluminum or other cheap dies makes this a useful method that can be set up for mass production—the discharge is repeatable within 30 seconds, especially where the spark is used. The method also has the advantage over the chemical explosive method that the shape and intensity of the shock wave can be more closely controlled, particularly with the vaporized wire. The disadvantage is the present very high cost of the electrical equipment involved.

Electromagnetic Forming

Very similar to the hydroelectric discharge method is electromagnetic forming (page 129). Once again the energy is stored in a bank of condensers and discharged suddenly, but this time the discharge is through a coil. This produces an intense and rapidly expanding magnetic pulse, which sets up sympathetic electrical currents in the workpiece. These in turn set up a magnetic field in opposition to the original field, and the interaction of the two sets up a force system that deforms the metal. In this technique the shape can be very closely controlled, and at the same time, by judicious shaping of the coil and of the magnetic field associated with it (using beryllium-copper field shapers), this control can be made very versatile. Once again, the main disadvantage of the system is the high cost of electrical equipment; and once again, the method can be used for the mass production of complex shapes in difficult metals. For very complex shapes, however, one-shot coils may be used and thrown away after each shot. (For mass produc-

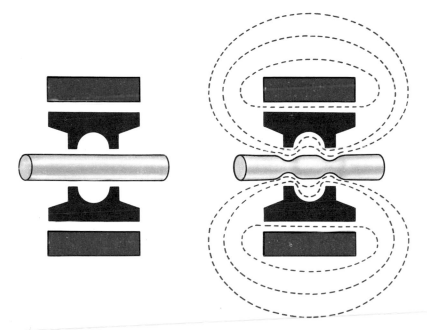

Electromagnetic forming. The magnetic field produced by the coil (red) and shaped by the pole-pieces (black) induces current in the workpiece (blue). The magnetic field associated with the induced current repels the original and shapes the metal.

tion the pressures produced have to be limited by the compressive strength of the coils rather than by the requirements of the component being shaped.) Dies can again be made from cheap materials, and in some cases may not even be required, since the magnetic fields can produce uniform, all-round pressures. The technique is particularly suitable for the shaping of sheet and for tubular parts, for swaging, and for the production of finned components. So far, commercial magnetic forming machines have produced only about 3×10^5 gauss, equivalent to 50,000 lb. per square inch, which is all right for copper and aluminum, but no good for a material like tungsten, which would need up to a million gauss—500,000 lb. per square inch.

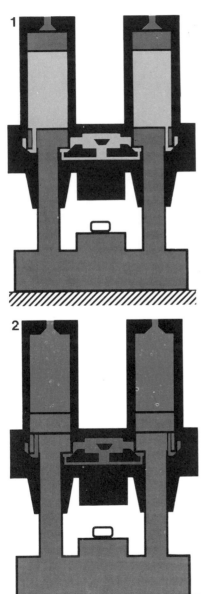

A " semi-explosive " high-energy-rate press. (1) The start of the cycle. (2) Hydraulic fluid (brown) moves the free pistons to compress the gas (blue). (3) The fluid pressure is released and the free pistons are driven back up by residual gas pressure; most of the gas, however, is trapped at high pressure in the central chamber, sealed by the lower pistons and the trigger (center). (4) The trigger is released and the gas moving through the trigger channel lifts the lower pistons far enough to break the seal, allowing the gas to raise the lower pistons with respect to the pressure chamber. (5) Both upper and lower parts of the device move and the impact is absorbed in the workpiece.

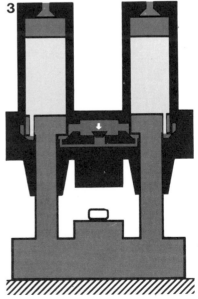

Pneumatic-mechanical Forming

For forging, forming, extrusion, powder compacting, shearing, and blanking, pneumatic-mechanical forming looks like developing into a useful mass-production technique. Here the rapid release of a high-pressure gas throws a free-acting piston against the workpiece at speeds of around 60 feet per second developed over a stroke of about 10–20 inches, giving work inputs of up to 500,000 foot-pounds. The series of diagrams on these pages shows the operating cycle of one such machine, developed by U.S. Industries Inc., in which the piston and anvil carrying the workpiece are both free-moving and are propelled toward each other simultaneously from a single release of gas. This counterblow action, as we saw in the case of the double-action explosive press for powder compaction produces a much greater energy input to the workpiece than would be possible with the conventional system of a hammer driven onto a stationary anvil. Also, because the piston and anvil are free-running, when they meet in mid-air there is no reaction on the frame, and the need for heavy foundations is removed.

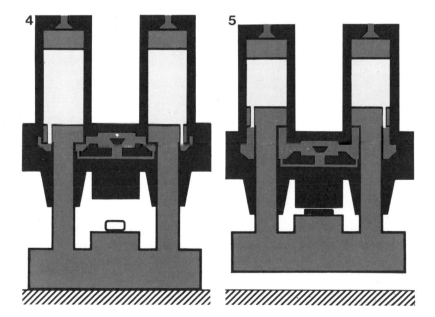

The most recent of these new high-speed forming processes to be developed is that using ultrasonic vibrations as the source of energy. In it a punch attached to a vibrator cycling at 20,000 cycles per second works against a static pressure holding the workpiece. The high speed allows deformation forces of about 30 times the holding force to be developed, yet with little or no friction. Stroke lengths are very short, and the process is best suited to dimpling of sheet, grinding, milling, and so on, where potentially it could give very great savings in time, plus much greater accuracy and less trouble from overheating.

High-energy-rate forming, then, while not completely revolutionizing all types of fabrication, adds a valuable range of new processes to the metallurgist's repertoire, allowing him to handle more metals economically than he could before, while at the same time he can do more with the traditional metals in the way of complex shaping, high accuracy, and the production of large components. Nevertheless, there are still many other possible areas of development; high-energy-rate forming cannot tackle all the shaping demands made by the engineer, nor has it yet eliminated the need for separately fabricated parts to be joined together. To fill these needs, a number of new and revolutionary machining and welding processes have been developed over the past few years, and no chapter on new ways for shaping metals would be complete without at least some mention of them.

New Machining Techniques

Traditional machining techniques make much use of the brute force of metal or ceramic on metal—one has only to look at any machine shop and see the turning, drilling, grinding, and so forth that goes on, and to notice the vast amount of waste developed, not only in the form of swarf, but as heat, to see that perhaps this is not the most sophisticated or efficient way of doing things. Look also at the vast amount of trouble that goes into making the right tools when really complex shapes have to be machined, and at the amount of time spent on regrinding tools, or on completely replacing them, because they cannot hold the necessary tolerances for more than a few operations at a time.

In the last few years metallurgists have begun to get around these troubles by harnessing the more basic and subtle powers of chemicals and electricity to do their machining for them. This has always been a possibility—and, as we shall see, some of the methods have in fact been in use for many years in very specialized applications—but in general their difficulties have far outweighed their advantages, to make them uneconomic compared with traditional mechanical techniques. Recently, however, the demands for much more complex and precise shapes and the need to use harder or more delicate materials (such as very thin foil) have spurred on improvements in these chemical and electrical techniques that have rendered them sound economic propositions in a great many important fields of machining.

Chemical Machining

The simplest of these processes is chemical machining, which is really a development of chemical and photoengraving techniques, in that a chemical is used to eat away the unwanted parts of the component, the rest being masked by an insoluble layer of, say, neoprene rubber. It was first introduced as a truly metallurgical process by American aircraft engineers faced with the growing problems of machining increasingly complex contours in airframe parts, both to meet the aerodynamic needs and as a means of saving weight by removing every possible unwanted piece of metal. Since then, the process and its modifications have found wide use in the aircraft and electronics industries, and are rapidly moving into many other fields of application.

Being a fairly slow process, chemical machining only becomes economic when very complex shapes are to be cut, or when the material to be machined is either very delicate, such as thin sheet, or exceptionally hard, so that mechanical methods would be even slower, assuming that they could be used at all. It is also a technique limited to quite shallow cuts, generally less than $\frac{1}{4}$ in. and not more than $\frac{1}{2}$ in. (for sheet being machined both sides at once). These limits are set largely by the inevitable sidecutting that occurs as the etchant eats its way below the mask. The surface finish produced is excellent—in fact, the process is often used simply to provide a good finish, especially on castings—while tolerances can be as close as 0·0002 in. One important advantage is that, because chemical machining can tackle metals of any degree of hardness, it can be used to finish off components that have already gone through all their stages of heat treatment; thus there is no danger of accuracy and shape being lost by scaling or distortion through having to perform hardening treatments after machining. Naturally there are great savings in tooling, while several components can be machined simultaneously, the number depending only on their size and the size of the available bath.

The basic technique is fairly simple: the component is sprayed with several layers of neoprene rubber, which is dried and cured; then, using a template, this mask is cut away in the appropriate places, before immersion in the etchant. A modification of this, developed in Britain and based on photoengraving, is used for cutting intricate hole patterns in very thin sheet. In this case a photosensitive mask is used, and an image of the pattern to be cut, when projected onto it, renders acid-resistant those areas to remain untouched. In this way extremely accurate, reproducible patterns can be machined in thin material that would otherwise be impossible, thus providing a production technique of great use for the complex demands of, in particular, the electronics industry.

Electron-beam Machining

Even finer than this is the use of a low-energy electron beam as the sensitizing medium, instead of light (see Chapter 8 below for a fuller discussion of the electron beam and its characteristics). In this case the component to be machined is coated with a liquid that can be transformed by the action of electrons and thus become soluble in the chosen etchant. By projecting an electron microscope image onto the coated component and the etching, very fine patterns indeed can be reproduced.

A second way of using an electron beam in this context is for direct cutting, in which a high-energy beam is used (the energy content being related to the cathode voltage). The high-energy concentration of such a beam, its extreme fineness, and the fact that its position can be closely controlled, make it ideal for close, complex pattern cutting, although its low penetration restricts its use to thin materials. Nevertheless, this too is an invaluable technique in making miniaturized electronic components.

Electrochemical Machining

Closely allied to chemical machining, but capable of removing much greater volumes of material economically—and, in particular, greater depths—is electrochemical machining. This is essentially electroplating in reverse, the important thing being to remove metal from the anode rather than to build it up on the cathode (in fact the process must be so designed that there is no buildup of material on the cathode, which is a closely shaped die). The general idea is to hold the die very close—0·03 in. or less—to the workpiece, both being immersed in an electrolyte, and to pass an electric current of sufficient density to remove material at a useful rate. The possibility of using such a process has been acknowledged for many years, probably since electrodeposition was originally developed, but until recently a number of inherent difficulties have made it less economical than conventional machining techniques. In the first place, the cathode must be moved up slowly as the workpiece is eaten away, and this involves the development of a delicate servomechanism that is sensitive not only to the gap between the electrodes, but also to the fluctuations

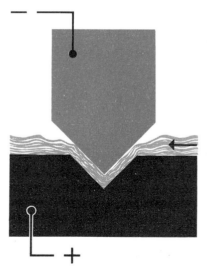

Electrochemical forming. The current ionizes metal from the positive side (workpiece). This metal passes into solution in the electrolyte, which is kept in motion to prevent buildup of concentration of metallic ions.

Electrochemical milling. The principle is the same as the electrochemical forming process, but the motion of the tool helps to keep the electrolyte in motion and sweeps away the debris.

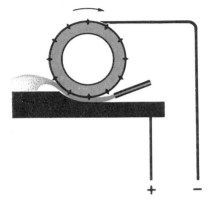

in electrical conductivity that take place in the electrolyte, which means that the actual necessary gap width varies throughout the machining process. At the same time the electrolyte must be kept moving rapidly between the electrodes to remove the metal debris as it is formed, which presents clear difficulties with so small a gap. And finally there is the danger that excessive local heating will take place in the gap, causing the electrolyte to evaporate rapidly. Only with materials that are particularly difficult to machine conventionally—mainly because they are hard, but also because the shape required is difficult—does electrochemical machining become economic.

The first important electrochemical machining devices to be developed were grinding wheels used for grinding carbide tools without any actual contact between the wheel (the cathode die) and the tool (the anode), although the wheel still rotated as in conventional grinding machines, dragging the electrolyte around with it. Though this method gives no particular advantage in production speed or accuracy, it does produce tools that are relatively stress-free—because they do not get hot during grinding and because there is no pressure on them from the wheel—which greatly reduces the incidence of cracking in service, and so effectively increases tool life.

Later developments contained the electrodes in a perspex box, thus giving better control of electrolyte flow, or arranged for the electrolyte to be pumped into the gap through the cathode itself. One of the first uses of the box technique was in the manufacture of turbine blades.

In general, though, the best applications of electrochemical machining are for the more delicate kinds of cavity, which would normally require the use of very small milling cutters, for which the rate of metal removal would be correspondingly slow.

Unfortunately, high accuracy is difficult to achieve with this technique, and each application needs a considerable amount of development time before the best combination of electrode shape, electrolyte flow, and so on is achieved. Even then it is quite impractical for tolerances of less than 0·005 in., and so is essentially an operation of particular usefulness for very hard materials.

Spark Machining

Maximum stock-feed rates for electrochemical machining lie between 0·02 and 0·2 in./min. For electrospark machining, on the other hand, which is the next process to be discussed and which, of these three processes, is probably the most important, feed rates can be as high as 0·5 in./min. Physically, electrospark machining looks rather like electrochemical machining, in that a shaped die is sunk into a workpiece, and between them is a moving fluid to carry away the debris. The difference lies in the fact that the fluid is a dielectric instead of an electrolyte, which means that it will not pass current until the voltage has reached a certain high level. When this voltage is reached by buildup in a condenser bank, a spark discharges across the electrode gap, removing metal from the workpiece.

As with electrochemical machining, electrospark machining becomes economic only when difficult materials and complex shapes are to be produced. Its main use, therefore, has come to be in the production of cavity dies for machine tools, and particularly for forging. Unlike electrochemical machining, the accuracy is very high, tolerances as close as 0·00015 in. being quite possible.

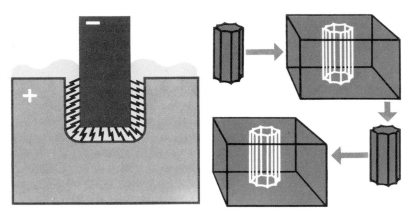

Spark machining. The metal is removed by a high-voltage discharge through a dielectric (nonconducting) fluid, which is kept in motion to remove the debris. The tools are expendable, and the actual tools used are copies of a master, reproduced by casting or powder compacting. Below: Spark machining in progress.

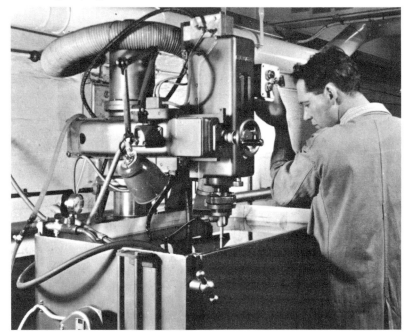

The starting point of spark machining is the manufacture of a master die by conventional machining, which then acts either as a forging die or as a casting mold, from which electrodes are made from fairly soft conducting materials such as zinc-tin alloy (the most popular), copper, brass, copper-tungsten, or cast aluminum (or sometimes metallized plastic). Thus, so long as several components are to be produced, say at least 3–5, electrospark machining can become economic. It can be used to cut any metal regardless of its hardness, or a heat-treated tool-steel die block, and there is no danger of distortion after machining because all heat treatment can be done previously.

Once again, as with high-energy-rate forming, these new machining methods are an important addition to the range already available; they can in no way be regarded as replacing the others, but simply as adding to their versatility. None of the processes is a new one. But new conditions and demands have made it worthwhile to find ways of overcoming some of their difficulties, and so make them economic in certain limited but important cases.

Electron-beam Welding

The third major field of fabrication, welding, is also undergoing fairly vigorous development, as one might expect. Most of this activity lies in modifying and improving the established techniques to cope with newer materials, to improve efficiency and speed of welding, and in automation.

The essentials of welding are the provision of a sufficiently intense source of heat, and its concentration in the right place. Everything else—the use of fluxes and of protective atmospheres, and the variety of heat sources, including oxyacetylene flames, the electric arc, electrical resistance, friction, and so on—are all subsidiary to these aims. To describe all the ways in which welding techniques are developing would probably bore the reader with unnecessary details. There is, however, one exciting new technique that is worth looking at; and in passing we might see some of the general problems the welding engineer has to face.

The process is electron-beam welding. A beam of accelerated electrons is obviously a very potent source of energy, for these tiny particles can be made to travel at speeds that are quite large fractions of the velocity of light. At the same time, because they carry an electric charge, they can be controlled very precisely, using magnetic fields. A simplified version of a device for generating and controlling a beam of electrons is shown on page 142. In practice the magnetic setup is much more complicated than this in order to give the necessary precise control. Using equipment of this kind, however, an electron beam can be focused on a piece of metal to produce a spot less than 0·01 in. in diameter, which gives a heat concentration 500 times as intense as that which is possible with conventional electric arc welding. Thus for the same temperature rise the energy input can be very low, while the area of metal that is actually melted is very small. This makes the process ideal for joining very small components, or for making very precisely located joints and pins. Another important advantage comes from the fact that the area of metal, other than that melted, that is actually affected by the heating is very small. In the first place this means that there will be little or no distortion and internal stressing caused by the inevitable expansion and contraction during heating and cooling; it also means that any actual metallurgical changes that occur during welding, and that can often cause trouble through the introduction of brittle or of soft phases, are restricted to an equally small area. Apart from the resulting improvement in welds made between pieces of the same metal, whether it could previously be welded or whether it was regarded as unweldable, as were many high-speed tool steels before electron-beam welding came along, this process also allows good welds to be made between many pairs of metals that were previously regarded as incompatible, because of their widely different thermal expansion coefficients or because of the complex metallurgical changes that occur when they are melted together.

Because control is so precise, welding conditions for electron-beam work can be very easily established and reproduced, which makes this one of the best welding processes for adaptation to mass production, especially where many small welds are needed in intricate components such as might be used in electronics.

Another advantage of electron-beam welding that we have not mentioned is the fact that, by the very nature of the equipment, welding must be carried out in a vacuum, for it is impossible to generate a controlled electron beam in the atmosphere, i.e. under any conditions where surrounding particles would interfere with the generation of electrons from the cathode. This means that the technique is particularly well suited to use on metals that are sensitive to small concentrations of gaseous impurities such as hydrogen, nitrogen, oxygen, which are liable to make them brittle. (If they are sensitive only to large quantities, then normal fluxes and protective atmospheres will do.) This applies particularly to many " modern " metals such as titanium, zirconium, tungsten, molybdenum, uranium, and so on, which is why the first use of electron-beam welding was in nuclear engineering, and why its main use remains there and in the electronics industry. The unfortunate restriction that comes from this, however, is that the size of components that can be welded is restricted to the size of available vacuum chambers; and it is a sad fact that vacuum chambers become rapidly more expensive as their size increases. There are

Spark machining. The photograph shows a small marking die (left) and the electrode used in forming it.

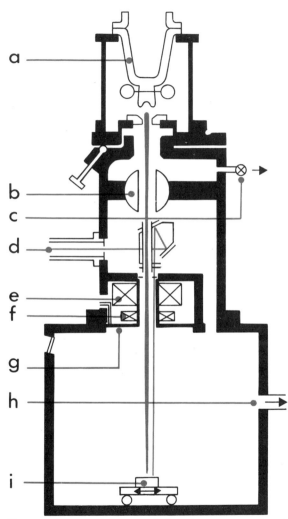

a

b
c
d

e
f

g

h

i

Electron-beam welding, carried out in a vacuum chamber. The position of the workpiece is servo-controlled ; the electron beam can also be deflected. The parts are : electron gun (a), column valve (b), column vent valve (c), optical viewing system (d), electron lens (e), deflection coil (f), water-cooled heat shield (g), connection to vacuum system (h), workpiece on movable table (i). The photo opposite shows material ·008 inch thick butt-welded by this process.

side effects also, such as the facts that complex remote controls must be provided to move the components about, and that lubrication under vacuum can be quite difficult, making such controls stiff. Devices such as a series of consecutive chambers, differentially pumped, with the last one open to the atmosphere, have been developed to allow the use of atmospheric electron-beam welding, but their advantages are marginal in other than exceptional circumstances.

Laser Techniques

Finally, a brief mention of lasers. Much has been said about the revolutionary possibilities of these intense sources of monochromatic light, and one of their obvious applications is in welding. For, like the electron beam, they provide a means of concentrating a large quantity of energy in a small area. Unfortunately the devices so far developed produce only intermittent pulses of

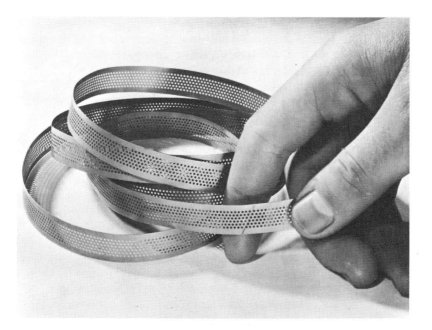

Electromagnetic energy can also be used in the form of light. The photo shows a laboratory setup for drilling 16-gauge aluminum with a 30-joule laser pulse of one millisecond duration.

energy, instead of the continuous (or very high frequency) supply that is preferable for most types of welding. Hence, at present at least, the laser is suitable only for small spot welds, and on the whole it seems unlikely to be better than electron-beam welding, for their energy output and control characteristics are very similar. In fact control of the laser beam, once produced, is less easy than control of an electron beam; a magnetic lens can have its characteristics changed almost instantly by suitable electrical manipulation, whereas a glass control lens must be physically removed and replaced if the focusing or direction of a light beam is to be changed. However, the light beam does have the advantage over all other welding heat sources that it can penetrate transparent solids, thus allowing components to be welded after they have been placed inside sealed glass chambers. In the electronics industry this could be invaluable.

So much for new ways of fabricating metals. This has not been an exhaustive survey; space would not allow it. But it has attempted to show some of the main processes being developed to supplement, if not to replace, our traditional techniques in order to meet the growing demands and changing economic conditions of the modern technological world.

7 Automation in the Metallurgical Industry

We are coming to a point in industrial development when automation is creating a revolution in methods and organization at least as great as that of the Industrial Revolution; and the metallurgical industry is feeling the impact of this no less than any other industry, and probably more than most. Metallurgical production is a capital-intensive activity, and thus automation is bound to be accepted more readily and initiated with more enthusiasm than in more labor-intensive industries, where it is cheaper to retain human operation and control than to replace it by elaborate electronic equipment. The position in the metallurgical industry is that large and complex machines are already run by a relatively few skilled workers; to automate is to improve efficiency considerably without affecting the labor force much either way, except perhaps to make life more congenial for them and to necessitate an increase in the number and quality of skilled maintenance engineers. In many places—in Sweden, for instance—computer automation is being introduced even though detailed economic analysis might

Partial view of a large modern steel works, giving some impression of the size and complexity of the operation.

not show an immediate advantage. The philosophy seems to be that it has got to come sometime, so it might as well be now.

The Possibilities of Automation

In considering the possibilities of automation it would be wrong to think of a metallurgical plant simply as a collection of furnaces, rolling mills, and forges, each to be provided with appropriate electronic gadgetry. Such a works is a single organic entity with one common and overriding aim—the production of metal to order at a profit. Thus, if the full benefits of automation are to be reaped the problem must be approached with a view to providing as fully integrated an automated unit as economic and technical considerations will allow. Modern technology already gives us the means to go a long way along this path, allowing us to automate not only a great many production processes, but also what have previously been regarded as almost exclusively the realms of human activity, namely, management, sales, accounting, finance, and so on, with many routine decisions being taken by computer (which, of course, can be overruled by the human manager, who uses them more as guidance than as practical decisions), leaving the planners free to make more creative and imaginative decisions based on a more effective flow of basic information than has ever been available previously.

Obviously it would be impossible in one short chapter to discuss adequately the whole subject of automation as applied in the metallurgical industry. We must be content with a typical example, a steelworks producing plate from the pig-iron stage upward, and, so far as processes are concerned at least, to two examples—the blast furnace and the plate-rolling mill.

The first thing that must strike any automation engineer on looking at these processes, as at any other metallurgical processes, is their essential unpredictability. So many factors are at work in each case that it is quite impossible, in the present state of affairs, to measure them all with any exactitude, even assuming one knows just what they all are. Even less feasible is the construction of any sort of viable mathematical model upon which to build a really permanent and inflexible automated system; even the basic settings around which the feedback mechanisms operate have to be

The control room of a modern electric furnace shop, mass-producing high quality alloy steels.

altered frequently to cope with changes in conditions in the furnace or mill such as lining- or roll-wear. Thus the automation engineer is faced with a " black box " situation—that is, he knows that if he does certain things at the input end, certain other things are likely to happen at the output end. But as yet he has very little useful knowledge about what goes on in between.

In the Blast Furnace

Of the two processes we shall discuss, the comments above are more particularly applicable to the blast furnace. The blast furnace of today is such a complex of interdependent variables that it is virtually impossible to build a mathematical model. Indeed, the main variables within the furnace, such as the temperature in various parts, the composition, speed, and pressure of the gas passing up the stack, the composition of iron and slag, the speed and pressure of the blast, the rate at which the burden is moving down the stack, and the distribution of the raw materials as they pass into the furnace, are all exceedingly difficult to measure and keep track of. And finally there is the expense and difficulty of providing automated equipment to handle the raw materials before they enter the furnace, ensuring that they are mixed in the right proportions, are of the right composition, and are spread evenly about the furnace top. Yet in spite of this a great deal of progress has been made in automating the blast furnace.

At present, varying the burden—i.e., the amount and kind of raw materials fed to the furnace—is the operator's primary means of furnace control. This has always been the main source of furnace control, for if the burden is not right, no amount of adjustment of other variables will produce the right quality of iron at the right temperature. On top of this, though, he must control the secondary factors such as the speed, moisture content, temperature, and gas content of the blast, or the pressure of the gas at the top of the furnace, all of which can affect the condition of the charge inside, and thus the rate and quality of the output of iron. For successful automation the blast-furnace manager must be given some way of presetting these controls, with the knowledge that the furnace will then behave as instructed without further attention, making its own adjustments and compensating as necessary. Already quite a number of furnaces throughout the world have been fitted with such preprogrammed automatic charging and automatic blast and pressure controllers.

Unfortunately this has proved too rigid a system for really successful operation, relying as it does on the assumption that the operator's choice of settings are correct, and that they will stay correct indefinitely. The trouble is that, because the available information about the process, and understanding of the process, are both far from complete, the way in which the operator expects his charge to behave, and thus the effects of his automatic settings, may be quite different from what is actually going on, so that even though the charge has been correctly mixed, weighed, and distributed, the furnace may not function at the optimum level all the time. At the same time, fluctuations in the behavior of the charge may not be detected for several hours—by observing changes in the iron produced—so that it never becomes immediately obvious that the settings need to be changed. Thus there is always a serious lag between the charge beginning to misbehave and the furnace control settings being adjusted to cope, by which time of course the charge may be behaving in yet another way, and so on. Even though the average blast furnace is capable of evening out a great proportion of the normal variations that one gets in a charge—variations in moisture content, particle size, and so on—most furnace operators agree that there is need for even more rigid control of the input, and that it is essential to get a faster control response to any fluctuations that do occur. To do this we must have methods for measuring charge material characteristics either continuously or very frequently, just before their entry into the furnace, and consequently of altering the settings continuously or very frequently.

In fact there is equipment in existence that allows us to do just this sort of rapid measurement. For instance, the chemical

Increasing sophistication of furnace control. In the system at top, quality and measurement of the product are the only criteria for adjusting furnace settings. The middle system exploits increased knowledge of furnace performance and improved measurement techniques to keep furnace parameters at present levels. In the bottom system, a computer compares furnace readings with past experience and continuously adjusts settings accordingly.

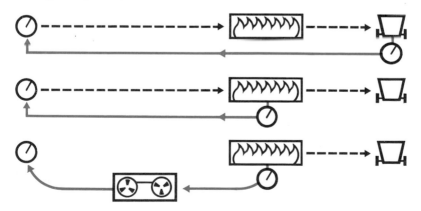

composition of the charge can be measured continuously using an X-ray device fitted at some suitable point in the loading equipment. (We shall be discussing the workings of X-ray analysis in the next chapter.) But this is a very expensive technique; economically more attractive, if less sophisticated, is to use ordinary chemical analysis of samples, but to carry them out in a special programmed analysis unit, which needs no help from the operator save programming and loading. A very important variable that is more difficult to measure is the charge moisture content. Water is deliberately added to the raw materials as they are being sintered; this is essential to give the right sintering conditions and so get sinter of the best lump size and porosity. The amount of moisture that subsequently goes into the furnace must be measured, and so far no good economical way of doing this has been found. In some cases it can be done by observing the behavior of the materials as they pass along the sintering strands, ensuring that particular temperature gradients prevail, which can, if other information is available, be related to moisture content. So far, though, the method has not become really established. Another technique is to bombard the charge with neutrons, which are slowed down or stopped by the hydrogen in the water; the degree of interference, and thus the moisture content, are measured on a scintillation counter. But again, the technique is not well proven, and anyway it is expensive. Various other methods are being tried, but so far none has really solved the problem.

The physical characteristics of the charge—the size and porosity of the lumps, in particular—also have a marked effect on its behavior inside the furnace. In this case, though, rather than devise methods for assessing these qualities, furnace operators are relying on the development of more careful controlling of sintering and pelletizing techniques to give a uniform and predictable product. This is much easier than measuring and making allowances for random variations.

Thus, even with available techniques, it is possible to give some degree of continuous charge measurement, and no doubt before long really comprehensive measurement will be possible, allowing automatic adjustment to give a consistent and balanced input. Given this the other controls become easier and more effective.

But even with this amount of control we are far from the ideal, for only experience and guesswork are ultimately behind us when it comes to knowing what is actually happening inside the furnace, and therefore the quality of iron likely to be produced. The furnace operator does not know that the adjustments he has set his equipment up to make are having exactly the effects he wants. This is an open-loop system. To close the loop, so that the controls can take account of events inside the furnace and adjust themselves accordingly, we need more detailed information on furnace conditions. This could then be fed into a computer to compare it with past experience of various furnace conditions and their results, and thus make the appropriate adjustments, which would be more subtle than anything possible with the present system. At the moment this is asking too much of our measuring capabilities and our knowledge of furnace reactions. But in several cases digital computers have been coupled with advanced measuring techniques to provide a fairly comprehensive record of internal furnace behavior, as accurately as it can be obtained (and, as might be expected, this accuracy is improving all the time). These systems are only one step away from full closed-loop control, and the conquest of what is probably the most complex of automation problems met with in the iron and steel industry.

Most of the industrial control development has centered around the raw-material input, the first priority being calculation of the required proportions of hot and cold metal, slagging additions, and the quantity of oxygen to be used. Later, however, more comprehensive analyses have been carried out, of which a typical example is that undertaken by the engineers of Lysaght's Limited, part of the United Steel Company in Britain.

The process they studied breaks down into nine component parts. First is the empty vessel containing some slag from the previous blow. Next a certain amount of scrap steel is added, and after that the main charge of hot iron. Next, a first blow takes place, in which oxygen and lime are blown through a lance onto the top of the molten iron. After this, some slag is run off, then blows are repeated until the required composition and temperature are reached, when the finished steel is run off. Now the vessel is ready for the next cycle and, as at the beginning, contains some residual slag. At any of these stages—before the metal is added to the vessel, during either of the blows, during the slag removal or teeming, or when the steel is in the ladle—nonmetallic additions can be made to adjust the composition precisely.

For full and effective automation, all the variables at all these stages must be known, recorded, and rapidly adjusted. The main things to be known in this case, in fact, were: the composition of the hot metal, and its temperature, the composition and temperature of the metal at the end of each blow, the ratio of hot metal to scrap, the slag composition for both blows, the quantities of oxygen blown, the distance of the lance above the melt, and the amount of slag held over between cycles, with its composition.

If the composition and weight of the metallic charge are known, then the required amounts of nonmetals such as lime, iron ore, and other fluxes can be calculated. These should all be worked out before charging, for speed is the essence of this process—at most it takes an hour to complete a cycle, and theoretically it can take as little as 35 minutes. If there are any errors or unpredicted behavior, then these will be discovered through the analysis at the end of the first blow and, provided something like rapid spectrographic analysis (see the next chapter) is used, corrections can be made.

Of course, we do not know exactly how the reactions go, and at what speed; as with the blast furnace, these adjustments from the outside cannot hope to give perfect results and, as in the case of the blast furnace, the aim must eventually be to use an on-line closed-loop computer system in which what is happening is compared to previous experience, and appropriate action taken. But first of all we have to gather the experience to build into the computer's memory, or rather the computer has to be given the experience with which to fill its own memory cells.

Toward this end the Lysaght's engineers decided to install a computer, which, while giving some degree of automatic control in the more rigid way, would also act as a data-logger, including the handling of spectrographic analysis, so as to build up a comprehensive understanding of the process to the level at which really effective closed-loop automatic control could be initiated.

Data-logging by computer in fact gives four main benefits in this case. First, it gives, as we have already said, a better understanding of the changes and reactions taking place during the course of a melting cycle; this is particularly valuable with a relatively new process such as this. Secondly, it provides a means of evaluating new techniques of control, either manual or automatic, as they are applied. Thirdly, it can provide a record of action taken and the instructions to operators. And finally, it allows the ultimate results—melt quality and temperature—to be correlated with accurate records of the associated processing.

All these are by way of preliminary advantages, preparing the ground for fully automated control. Thus at present the computer system operates rather as follows. From the target specifications for the end of the first blow and the latest temperature and analysis figures for the hot metal, the charge quantities are calculated, including allowances for as many variables as possible, according to the current state of knowledge. The results of these calculations are displayed by the computer to the operators, who can then either act on them or ignore them at will, the recommended and actual quantities charged being automatically logged. Target specifications can be reset at will by the operator, and new calculations made accordingly.

This is far from the ideal of fully automated control, and there is a great deal of data-gathering to be done before that state is reached. But the amount of progress that has been made so far in mastering the two vastly complex processes of iron-making and steel-making shows that the goal is well within our reach.

In the Rolling Mill

Our second example, the plate rolling mill, is somewhat different in essence from the blast furnace in that there are no complex chemical reactions to be allowed for, and it is much more open to a strict mathematical analysis. Nevertheless this analysis, and the construction of a control system around it, are complex exercises. At the same time many of the rolling variables are just as difficult to measure in line as are furnace variables, so that automation of rolling is in effect no less difficult a task than those we have already described.

Producing a steel plate is not a simple task of putting a slab of metal through a set of rollers until reduced to the right thickness, then cutting it up to the widths and lengths ordered by customers. Most slabs that arrive at the plate mill are cold, so first they must be heated to the right temperature for rolling, in a slab-reheating furnace. After this they go once through a special heavy mill whose job is not to produce any change in dimensions but simply to break up the scale that has formed on the slab surface. (Quite often high-pressure water is used instead of rollers at this stage.) Next the slab passes into the roughing mill. The general effect of any mill is to reduce the thickness of whatever is passing through it, while extending the length, but leaving the width—the dimension parallel to the rollers—virtually unaffected. Usually when rolling plate the width of the slab is extended to form the finished width (although sometimes the length is used) so that after a few initial passes in the roughing stand to extend the length a suitable amount (depending on the required final dimensions) the slab is turned through 90° and rolled until the required width dimension is reached. Now it is turned again through 90° and rolled further until the thickness has been reduced enough to allow it to pass on to the finishing stand. The job of this stand is to produce the final specified thickness uniformly throughout the length and breadth of the plate, which should also be as level as possible, with no alteration in the width and little change in length. Some mills have small vertical edging rollers to ensure that the plate width does not increase. After this stage the plate may be heat-treated to remove any internal stresses that have built up, and to adjust its structure; then it is passed through a set of leveling rollers to remove any kinks still left, finally passing to the cooling banks where, as soon as it is cool enough to be worked on, it is marked, cut, and stacked for dispatch.

Human operators coping with such a situation obviously rely a great deal on accumulated experience—rules of thumb, observation, and judgment, aided by whatever simple instruments can be provided. The crucial man in all this is the actual rolling-mill operator controlling the passage of metal through the rollers. With information from the soaking pits, or, if he is operating the finishing mill, from the roughing-mill operator, on the estimated temperature, size, and required final dimensions of the material coming to him, he sets the pressure and separation of his rollers in expectation that the metal will behave in an average manner. After the first pass he can tell whether or not this is so—whether the steel is softer or tougher than he expected—and so calculate his mill settings for the next pass. All this he must do swiftly and accurately, with what is in fact a very limited amount of information.

When we consider the great variety of dimensions (width, length and thickness) of orders, and the many different types of steel specified, all with different properties, it is easy to see how complex the control task in the rolling mill really is. In addition, the behavior of a piece of metal between the rollers varies not only with its composition, but also with its temperature, which in turn alters at different rates according to the volume and surface area of the slab, the temperature of the rollers, and so on; while variations come about in the shape of the rollers themselves as the result of temperature variation and wear. Indeed, in some rolling mills two pieces of steel of the same composition and dimensions are quite rare. The layman may well be surprised that any piece of finished steel is ever the right size except by sheer luck. When we add to these the difficulty of continuously measuring temperature and dimensions accurately, the task, once again, begins to look insuperable. Even the apparently simple job of measuring the temperature of the slabs as they leave the reheating furnace is complicated by the existence of a scale of unknown thickness that makes the usual optical methods difficult to apply.

In considering automation the sequence must be considered as a whole, from reheating to dispatch of finished plate. At each stage the conditions must be so adjusted that the product coming out is within a defined set of tolerances for receipt by the next stage, although the system must not be so inflexible that it cannot cope with material outside specification. And not only must automation control the proper operation of each process, but it must also plot a careful schedule for the plates passing through the sequence of operations, so as to make the optimum use of each of its parts.

Automatic control of the transport of material between stages of the process presents no great difficulties, since most works already have motorized continuous transfer equipment, and the main problems are likely to be concerned with route and timing. The later stages of the process, too, present no great difficulties apart from scheduling—techniques for automatic heat-treatment, leveling, cutting, inspection, and even dispatch (which is really a problem of correct stocking and recovery) are all quite well developed. The main problems have arisen around the rolling mills themselves, which is where conditions are changing most rapidly.

As with furnace investigations, most of the initial investigation work in this field has been concerned with comprehensive logging of data about the main variables, from which it has been possible to make calculations about the optimum mill conditions, and from these to work out the necessary control systems. As a result, a great deal of progress has been made in mill automation, both in Europe and in the United States, although in most cases the innovations are far from complete automation of the whole system, for there are still gaps in technique as well as in knowledge.

One of the earliest plate mill computer systems was that designed by Westinghouse for the Republic Steel Corporation. From a punched-card input of basic instructions and from measurements made automatically during rolling, the computer can control roll and speed settings on a scale breaker, a single-pass roughing stand, and the finishing stand. In addition, it controls the speed settings of the approach and delivery tables, and all its actions are initiated by signals from hot-metal detectors that determine the position of the workpiece at any instant.

After the slab has passed through the scale breaker, which in this case also gives some reduction, its width is known accurately. From this, the known weight of the slab, and its assumed density, the computer calculates the thickness to give the required slab length, which, after turning, will be the finished plate width. If possible the single-pass roughing stand is set to give this width (taking into account apparent slab temperature, roll shape, and all those other variables we have already discussed) so that the slab can be turned and rolled to the finished thickness as soon as it arrives at the main stand. If the right dimensions are not obtained, then the computer makes appropriate adjustments.

Since the installation of this system, other plate mill computers have gone into service. None of them provides a complete automation system taking all variables into account. But, as with the furnaces, they provide a working basis for further development.

In Combined Processes

As we have already suggested several times in this chapter, automation, particularly of anything so complex as a metallurgical works, cannot simply be a case of automating individual pieces of equipment. No metallurgical plant is just a collection of furnaces, mills, and forges. Such a works is a single organic whole, and it must be treated as such. It would be useless to improve the quality and output of pig iron from a blast furnace if this led to queues of ladles and ingots jostling around the steel furnaces (or, what in fact would happen, a great increase in stocks of cold pig). And the same applies to any other part of the plant. The total operation of a works, be it producing steel, aluminum, copper, or any other metal, is complex and interdependent, so that any slight change in one part—any breakdown or holdup, or any speedup through automation—is bound to have repercussions throughout the rest of the system, and for some time into the future. Such off-balance has to be corrected by the skill of the operators and planners. In addition, we must remember that the processes themselves are evolving, a particularly important tendency being toward integration and streamlining. The most important development of this kind at the moment is continuous casting, in which molten metal is poured from ladles, or even direct from its furnace, into a casting device that converts it into finished sections or plate. In a steel-works such as the one we have been describing this cuts out a vast sequence of operations including the casting of ingots, their removal from the molds, and passage through the soaking pits, scale-breakers, and roughing- and finishing-mills. Elaborate and expensive automation of unintegrated plant will obviously form a reactionary barrier against such developments if the possibility of their introduction as an alternative course, now or at some time in the near future, is ignored. No matter how much automation of individual parts of the process we carry out, the ideal aim will always be a singe piece of plant that takes in ore and fuel at one end and turns out fully finished material at the other, with no intermediate transfer or waiting stages. At the same time, a works rarely produces one standard product. It produces perhaps hundreds of different grades, in many hundreds of different sizes and shapes, and almost invariably to customers' strict orders. All these orders

A modern hot-strip mill. The hot steel strip at the end of the mill, which may be up to four feet wide and half an inch thick, moves at up to forty miles an hour, but the dimensional tolerance on rolls must be continuously controlled to thousandths of an inch.

have to be scheduled through the plant, from raw materials input at the stockyards to the dispatch bay, so that each is delivered in the optimum time, to the right quality standards, with the least delay and congestion within the mill. But none of this scheduling can be planned very far in advance. Even if every production and transfer rate were known exactly, the system is far too complex even to build a mathematical model with which to feed a planning computer. When you add to this the fact that the exact quantity and quality of, say, iron coming from the blast furnace, or steel coming from a converter, are unknown until they actually arrive—and even then not until they have been poured into ingots—or that the exact behavior of an ingot in the rolling mills cannot be known until it is actually being rolled, and that this sort of uncertainty persists throughout the works, it is clear that, on the one hand, preplanned scheduling is quite impossible, while on the other hand some kind of dynamic scheduling that makes decisions on the spot according to prevailing conditions—like an experienced human scheduler, but faster, and able to examine more possibilities—is just as essential an innovation as would be full closed-loop automation of every main process. And on top of all this there are the various administrative and development departments—the laboratories, order and dispatch departments, sales and marketing, accounts, wages and salaries, forward planning, and so on—in fact, all the departments associated with any commercial enterprise. All of them are being shown to be capable of benefiting from the use of computers, not just for doing sums, but for tackling real comprehensive planning and decision problems.

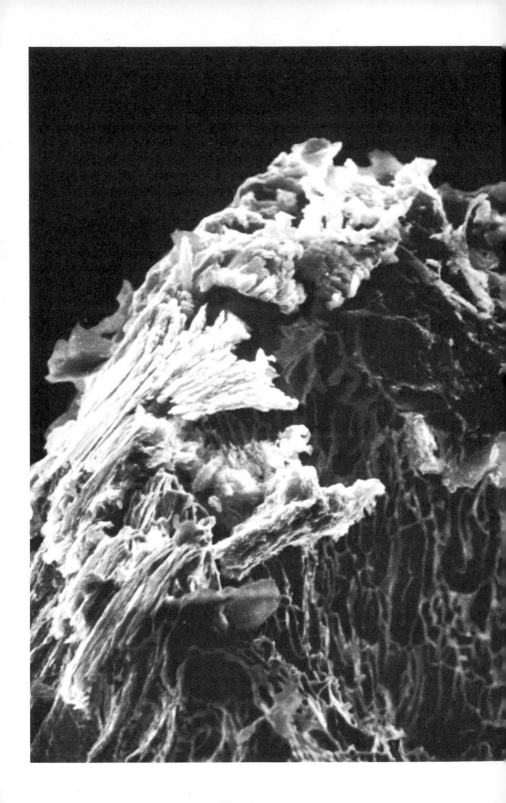

8 Modern Ways of Examining Metals

The properties of modern metals and their alloys are probably more sensitive to slight changes in composition and internal structure than any other nonliving materials. Certainly this is true from a practical viewpoint; we have already seen several times in this book how sensitive properties can be to even very slight changes in composition. And there are many cases where the accidental presence of only a few hundredths of one per cent of impurity ruins the performance of an alloy. In the earlier chapters we saw something of the fundamental importance of structure—of the extreme dependence of behavior on the shape and nature of internal features, and how the very nature of metals springs from their unique kind of crystallinity.

In view of this it is hardly surprising that techniques for investigating composition and structure are among the most important of the metallurgist's tools, whether he is working on fundamental research into metal physics, or as a furnace manager. Nor is it surprising to find that over the years metallurgists have continually

Microphoto (×830) of ductile fracture in soft iron wire. The photo was taken using an electron microscope.

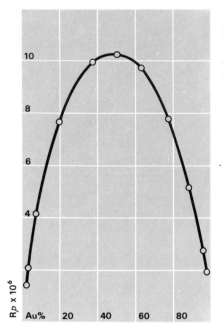

Specific electrical resistance of gold-silver alloy as a function of proportion of gold. The variation over the range 0–100 per cent is over threefold. The other properties of alloys vary even more sharply with small changes in composition.

taken advantage of the latest methods, so that today they are regular users of the most advanced and sophisticated techniques and equipment. Where high accuracy is needed (the ability to identify impurities present as only a few parts per million, or to give analyses correct to a hundredth of one per cent or less), or speed (giving in a few seconds an accurate analysis of an alloy containing a dozen or more elements), or, for structural examinations, very high resolutions and magnifications (the ability to investigate the arrangement of the atoms themselves, or to " see " features only a few thousandths of a millimeter across), then up-to-date techniques using X-rays, electron beams, or field-ions are essential.

The Range of Techniques

A look at the diagram opposite will show you the main physical techniques available to the metallurgist. Chemical methods of analysis are much less common now and do not warrant much discussion here; they are far too slow and complex to be of real use

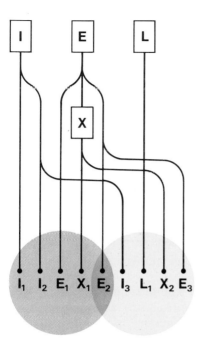

Families of methods of examining metals. The major methods are: ionization techniques (I), electron-beam techniques (E), which give rise to X-ray techniques (X), and light microscopy (L). The major objectives of examination are compositional analysis (blue circle) and structural analysis (yellow circle). The techniques are: optical spectrometry (I_1), mass spectrometry (I_2), electron-beam fluorescence (E_1), X-ray fluorescence (X_1), electron-beam scanning microanalysis (E_2), field-ion microscopy (I_3), light microscopy (L_1), X-ray crystallography (X_2), electron microscopy (E_3).

to metallurgists except in a few cases. The principle is simple enough: Find and apply the right sequence of chemical reactions to tell you, without ambiguity, what elements are present. Knowing this, you can apply another set of mutually exclusive reactions to find out what proportions of the various components are present. Only the practice is complex, as you can imagine, with so many possible combinations of elements and reactions.

The two zones marked in the diagram represent the two main fields of analysis—compositional and structural—with which the metallurgist is concerned, and the techniques associated with them. As you will see, one of these techniques—electron-scanning microanalysis—can cope with both types of analysis, while the two classes of technique based on ionization and on the use of the electron beam both produce techniques of either kind. The use of light, on the other hand, generates only one technique, the metallurgical microscope, which, although now superseded in many ways, has provided the backbone of structural metallurgy.

The Metallurgical Microscope

For many years this was the only technique available for investigating metal structures, and even now it is the metallurgist's most valuable piece of equipment for everyday use, allowing him to investigate the general arrangement and size of grains, the existence of internal deformation, the large-scale distribution of phases, fractures, and other faults, and the presence of segregations of impurities or alloying constituents. When he needs to see details finer than can be shown up by a magnification of one or two thousand times, the metallurgist will have to resort to other methods; but for the bulk of structural work a good optical microscope backed by years of accumulated experience can yield a great deal of invaluable qualitative information of the kind already described. The foundations of modern structural metallurgy have been built on the knowledge gained from this instrument, and it is certainly not a has-been now that so many more sophisticated techniques are available.

Even so, the optical microscope has serious limitations for those wanting to carry out the more detailed and fundamental investigations of structure—the structure of minute particles and grain boundaries, for instance—that are so important to modern alloy development. The most important of these faults is the relatively low magnification that can be obtained, even from the very best instruments. Then there is the fact that the microscope cannot identify what it is looking at, except by the experience of the observer, and it cannot give any compositional analysis of features.

Fundamentally the optical microscope is limited in application by the fact that the wavelength of light is so much greater than the average distance between individual atoms; it is impossible to see with any clarity any feature smaller than that wavelength, or even several times larger. Some sort of analogy can be got from thinking of using an unmarked foot-rule as a measuring instrument. To measure a thimble with it would be a pretty inaccurate affair. Measuring things of the order of one foot would still involve a considerable amount of guesswork. Only objects with dimensions of several feet could be measured with any reasonable accuracy. On the other hand it would be a tedious job to measure up the Forth Bridge with such a rule—so it is no good using very high-powered techniques (such as the X-rays we shall be talking about in a moment) to do the large-scale investigations that the optical microscope has been coping with so well for so long.

Von Laue's Crucial Experiment

As you will see on page 165 the most fruitful class of analysis technique is that based on the use of the electron beam, either directly or after transformation to X-rays. Although most of the techniques are of quite recent origin, their basis goes back to a historic experiment suggested by the German physicist Max von Laue and actually carried out by two of his research students in 1912. It was the meeting point of two quite separate lines of thought and, as so often happens in such cases, its results were explosive.

At that time scientists knew well enough that metals were crystalline. What they did not know was the internal nature of crystals. For some years, however, the idea first put forward by Ludwig Seeber in 1824, that crystals consist of layers of atoms distributed in regular patterns, had been widely accepted. In the 1890s mathematicians had even worked out all the ways in which atoms could possibly be distributed inside a crystal. But there was then no direct experimental evidence in support of these ideas.

In a completely different area of physics, scientists were worrying about the nature of X-rays, which had been discovered about 30 years previously. The majority were convinced that these rays were actually waves like light, although with a much shorter wavelength. But here again, no experiment had successfully confirmed or refuted this idea.

What von Laue did was to suggest a single, simple experiment to test both ideas at once. He reasoned that if X-rays were very short waves, with lengths of the order of an atomic spacing (which everyone assumed to be very very small indeed), and if a crystal was a three-dimensional space lattice of atoms, then a thin beam of X-rays, on passing through a crystal, would undergo diffraction and produce a characteristic pattern on a photosensitive plate. Thus, if the experiment did indeed give this result, the atomic hypothesis of crystals and the wave theory of X-rays would be confirmed simultaneously.

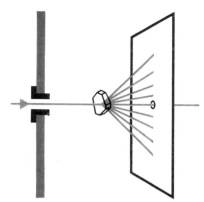

Left: Setup of von Laue's original experiment. A beam of "white" X-rays is diffracted through a single crystal of rock salt to produce a distinct pattern on a sensitive plate.

Opposite: Cancellation of waves related randomly in phase. At point A, the red lines show positive amplitude above the line, negative below. Only the special cases where the waves are all in phase give reinforcement.

The diagram on this page shows how the experiment was finally set up. Basically it was very simple. A pencil of X-rays was directed onto a single crystal and then passed onto a photographic plate. If von Laue was right the rows of atoms would act as a diffraction grating for the minute waves and, besides the spot formed by the main beam, there would be other spots around it formed by the diffracted beams. And in fact this is just what happened when the students of von Laue, Friedrich and Knipping, carried out the experiment; a complex but symmetrical pattern of spots was formed on the plate. Repeats of the experiment with different types of crystal showed that each one formed its own characteristic pattern. Thus a technique for examining the structure of crystals was born, which, as X-ray crystallography, has become one of the foundation stones of the materials sciences, including metallurgy as we saw in Chapter 1.

X-ray Diffraction

Before we can discuss the ways in which the idea can be used to extract information about metallic crystal structures, we need to know briefly why it works as it does.

Imagine, then, a single atom being struck by a high-energy wave front such as an X-ray (or, at this point in the argument, it could be a beam of light). Energy from the beam will be absorbed by the atom, some of whose outer electrons will become excited and move to higher energy levels. In this state they are unstable, and after a

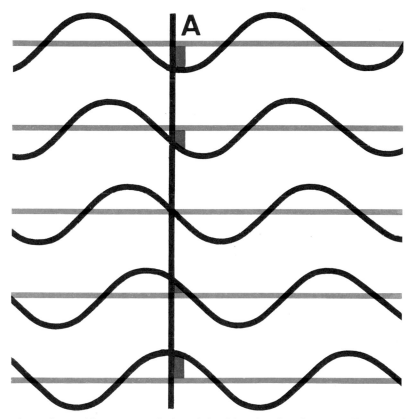

short time will revert to their original level, releasing new X-rays of various wavelengths as they do so. However, a certain amount of the incident energy is simply bounced off the nucleus and emerges unaffected, forming a secondary wave front of the same wavelength as the incident beam. Further, the phase of the reflected wave is systematically related to the phase of the incident wave.

Now suppose that instead of a single atom, the beam strikes a row of atoms of the same material. Once again each atom will scatter the beam, thus producing a series of spherical wave fronts that will now interfere with one another. The result of this will be to produce a new beam in a direction that depends upon the wavelength of the original beam, the angle at which it strikes the row of atoms, and the distance between the atoms (which in real life will be virtually the same for each pair).

We can extend this argument to a three-dimensional lattice, with similar results: That the incident beam will be scattered by the atoms of the plane or lattice, that interference will occur, and that, under the right conditions, a new beam will be produced. If we were to examine the interference closely, we should find that a diffracted beam could only be produced when the beam struck the planes of atoms at certain rigidly defined angles (the values of which are given by a simple formula known as Bragg's Law, which we need not go into here). In a single crystal all the planes of a given kind are parallel and, of course, there is no guarantee that our beam will

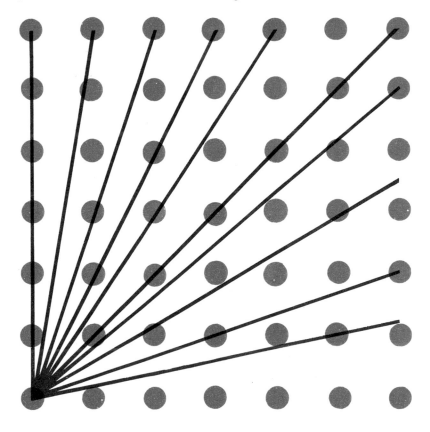

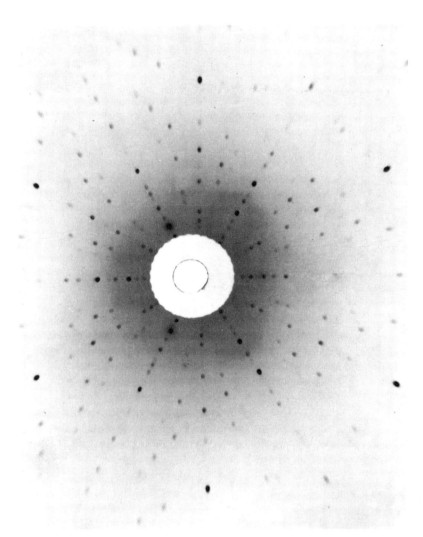

Opposite : The black lines show the main diffraction planes in the patterns of blue dots.

Above : Typical X-ray diffraction pattern for a single crystal, in this case of silicon. The crystallographer can deduce the basic structure of the crystal from the pattern of dots.

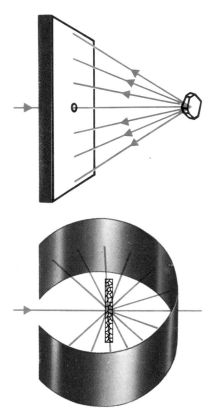

Setup for back-reflection X-ray crystallography techniques for measuring orientation. The method is often used in machining single crystals for the electronics industry.

Another important X-ray technique used in detailed studies of alloy systems. The specimen is made up from powdered metal on polycrystalline wire, and the whole range of diffraction is examined to determine what crystal structures are present.

strike them at a critical angle. To ensure this we have to rotate the crystals about a vertical axis: The planes will thus pass through all the critical angles and a number of diffracted beams will be produced, forming their characteristic spots on the photographic plate. Alternatively we could do what von Laue's students did and use a beam of X-rays of a whole range of wavelengths, instead of the monochromatic beam used today, thus guaranteeing that there would be a wavelength appropriate to the angle of our crystal.

The intensity of the spots and their relative positions depend on the distance between the various planes of atoms (the diagram on page 170 shows that in a single crystal there are several planes that can have their effect) and on the crystal structure.

Practical metals are almost always polycrystalline, and X-rays would be of little use if they could not be used to investigate this condition. But in fact they can be and are, for in a piece of polycrystal there are bound to be many planes at critical angles, and so once again a pattern can be produced, this time without the need for rotation of the specimen. Again, crystal structures can be determined, and such things as distortion and internal stress and preferred orientation can be studied. There are several variations in technique, each of which has particular advantages for various kinds of investigation. They are shown on page 172.

The Production of X-rays

So far we have said nothing about the actual production of X-rays. This might not be important here if it were not fundamental to the next technique we are to talk about. Most readers will already have come across the idea that atoms can be induced to emit electromagnetic radiation by suitable excitation of their electrons to energy levels higher than their normal level, followed by a sudden return to stability. The greater the excitation the shorter is the wavelength of the new radiation, until eventually, with excitation by high-speed electrons or hard (short-wavelength) X-rays, we get X-rays produced. We have already seen this mechanism at work in making possible X-ray diffraction, and on page 174 we show a simplified X-ray tube, in which high-speed electrons stimulate X-ray production from a metal target.

Two forms of X-rays may be produced. The first is a continuous range of wavelengths, known as " white " X-rays, with a definite limit at the short-wavelength end of the spectrum. As the voltage of the cathode is raised the energy content of the electron stream rises, and this short-wavelength limit falls, as does the peak wavelength.

When a certain cathode voltage, critical for each target material, is exceeded, the second kind of radiation is produced, in which there are marked increases in the intensities of certain wavelengths. The important thing about this is that the exact wavelength that becomes intensified depends upon the particular element forming the target. Usually there are several such wavelengths, but the most important and the most intense are known as K-alpha and K-beta radiation.

Below : Setup for a typical device for producing X-rays. Electrons (A) from the hot cathode (B) strike the target (C), which consists of metal especially chosen for the wavelength required. The target is cooled by means of a water-cooling system (D). Interaction of electrons with the target produces X-rays (E) that pass out through vacuum-sealed metal windows (F). The voltage of the electrons, and therefore the characteristics of the X-rays, is controlled by means of the electrical system (G).

Opposite : Wavelengths of X-rays shown as a function of voltage. A range of wavelengths is produced (left) with a peak moving to the lower end as voltage increases. Eventually a critical voltage is reached at which the target produces the characteristic single wavelengths used to identify the metal. A sample scan of steel (below) shows the characteristic wavelengths produced by the various constituents.

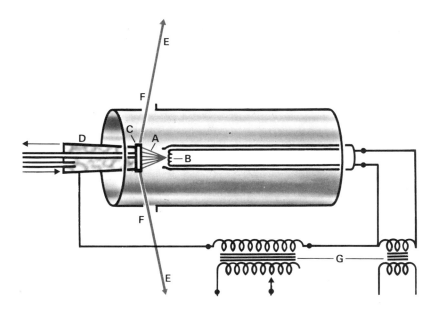

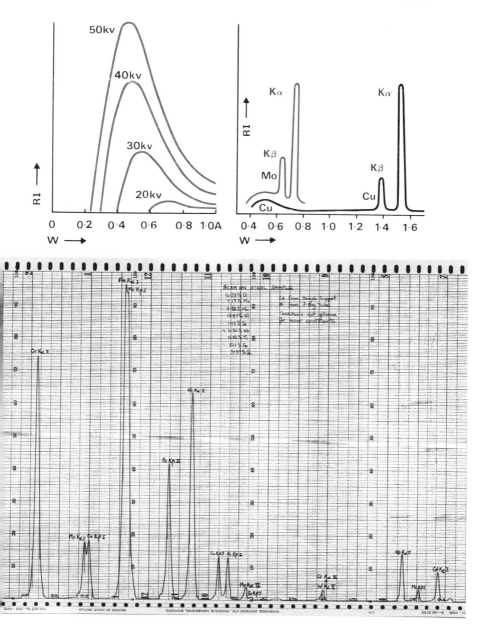

Analysis from Characteristic Wavelengths

It must be obvious that here is a simple way of identifying elements; all we have to do is to bombard our specimen with electrons above the critical voltage, measure the wavelengths of the characteristic radiations produced and compare them with a list of standards. And in fact this is exactly the basis of X-ray spectroscopy, a rapid, accurate analysis technique of great importance in the research laboratory and in industrial production.

One of the great advantages this technique has over chemical analysis methods is that each element produces its characteristic radiation irrespective of what other elements are present, whereas chemical analysis requires a different, specific test for each element. Also, having sorted out the characteristic wavelengths, by measuring their relative intensities we can calculate the percentage of each element present, thus using one physical result from one test to give us two kinds of information. Even allowing for the time taken to produce the specimens in a form suitable for use as a target (it has to be powdered and pressed onto a standard target, or made into a solution and painted on), to mount the target inside the vacuum tube, and to process the film (although counting devices can be used instead of film), five- or six-fold savings are easily achieved on the simpler standard analyses, and much greater savings on others. One common analysis, for instance, is the determination of the amounts of iron and chromium in steels. By wet chemical methods this takes a chemist about three and a half hours. X-ray spectroscopy takes half an hour over the job, and is at least as accurate.

Nevertheless, useful as it is as a research tool, the direct-emission X-ray spectrograph, as this device and its variants are called, has a number of snags that have held back its widespread use as a method of industrial inspection. Although, when compared to chemical analysis, it is a rapid technique, it is not rapid enough for use in a works where the operation of a process awaits the results; in this respect the optical spectrograph (which we shall be talking about later) is faster. Specimen preparation is troublesome because, while it is bombarded under vacuum, it tends to decompose, or suffer from selective evaporation, in which some more volatile components are lost, thus leading to inaccuracy. The difficulties associated with the type of X-ray tube that can be opened up to insert the specimen were another important factor in its relative failure as a production line technique. Most of the difficulties described have been overcome in the X-ray fluorescent spectrometer.

The X-ray Fluorescent Spectrometer

In this instrument the characteristic X-ray emission is induced by bombarding the specimen with short-wavelength X-rays instead of with electrons. This immediately removes the troubles associated with having to put an especially prepared specimen inside a vacuum tube; a small piece of the metal under test can be cut and mounted outside the X-ray tube, the exact form of the sample being unimportant. The production of X-rays can now be much better controlled, for there is no need to compromise with the requirements of a demountable tube (as the tube for the direct-emission

The diagram shows an X-ray fluorescent spectrometer of the type used in metal analysis. X-rays produced by the tube (A) strike the specimen (B), producing a scatter of characteristic X-rays (C). These are collimated at (D) and pass through a crystal (E) and a further collimator (F) to reduce unwanted " background " rays. The intensities and wavelengths of the characteristic X-rays are then measured at (G) in the case of low-intensity rays and at (H) for those of higher intensity.

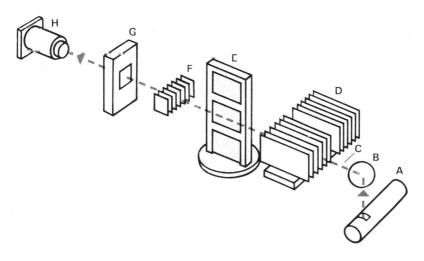

The console unit of a typical industrial X-ray fluorescent spectrometer.

spectrograph is called). Although this system is less efficient than the other, in that it produces a smaller signal for the same power input, very high-powered tubes can be used, and by using modern counting devices, which are about 1000 times more sensitive than film, much more can be learnt from the signal.

In recent years, then, the X-ray fluorescent spectroscope has become an important addition to the range of analysis techniques. With programmed operation and high-speed counting, commercial equipment can be set up to give analyses covering 14 or more elements all at the same time, within a matter of minutes—simply open the specimen holder, drop in the specimen, switch on, and wait for the results to click up on the recorder, accurate to one tenth of a percent or better.

The Electron Microscope

So far, in discussing the use of electrons to study metals we have mentioned only their indirect use, as a source of X-rays. The electron microscope, however, uses them directly to form an image in much the same way that the optical microscope uses light. But, because the wavelength of electrons is so much smaller than that of light they can provide very much higher resolutions and magnifications. The electron-microscope is thus a highly potent device for the visual examination of very fine structural detail in metals, as well as of other materials.

Glass is opaque to electrons, so that glass lenses cannot be used to focus them. However, being electrically charged, they can be controlled by magnetic fields, as we have already seen in discussing the generation of X-rays, and as anyone with even a little knowledge of the workings of a television set will know. Using such a focusing system, resolutions of 10 A or less can be obtained (the average atom has a diameter of about 1 A, which is 10^{-8}cm.), while the general resolution is around 50 to 200 A, which is considerably worse than the best theoretical resolution. Most of the limitation comes from the fact that, like glass lenses, magnetic lenses suffer from defects such as spherical and chromatic aberration. The former gives rise to different amounts of bending of the rays across the radius of the lens, while the latter is due to the different amounts of bending caused by rays of different wavelength. In a glass lens they cause uneven focusing and coloring of the edges of the image, and the effects in a magnetic lens are exactly analogous. To overcome them, very small lens apertures must be used, which

The " optical " system of the electron microscope (bottom), though many times more powerful, is basically the same as that of the light microscope (top). In the latter, glass lenses focus light waves, and in the former, magnetic " lenses " focus an electron beam. Both consist of a condenser lens (A), an objective lens (B), and an eyepiece (C).

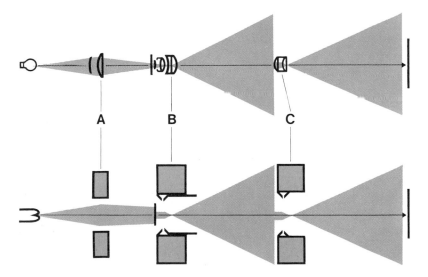

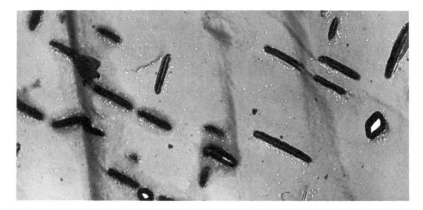

Above: Age-hardening precipitate of copper-aluminum compound can be seen interfering with lines of dislocation in this electron photograph (×30,000) of an alloy consisting of aluminum and 4 per cent copper.

Below and opposite: Four techniques for making replicas of metal surfaces for examination under the electron microscope. (a) The method used for aluminum. The red line is an oxide skin produced by anodizing, which can then be peeled off, providing an accurate replica thin enough to pass electrons. (b) An impression of a hard alloy such as steel is made in soft aluminum, from which a replica can be made by method (a). (c) A thin layer of silver plated onto the specimen surface is isolated by dissolving away the base metal. This is then used to produce a transparent plastic replica. (d) For heightened contrast, replicas can be " shadowed " by spraying with gold or other electron-opaque metal.

a

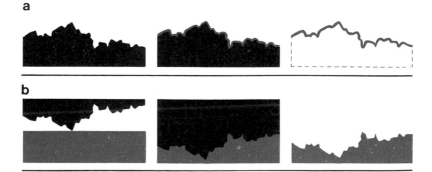

b

tend to cut down resolution, although giving good depth of focus. In fact this last can be very much better than is possible with any optical microscope because the high intensity of the electron beam allows very much smaller apertures to be used.

Specimens may be viewed in the electron microscope by reflection of the beam from their surface, just as in an optical metallurgical microscope. But the usual method is to use transmitted radiation, as in the biological microscope, in which the light shines up through a very thin specimen. Because electrons are easily stopped by matter this means that the specimens used are very thin—500 to 1500 A—and are in fact replicas of the polished and etched surface of the metal specimen (which gets around the difficulty of cutting a metal specimen down to such an extremely small thickness). The replicas copy the contours of the surface, and the contrast in the image arises from the different thicknesses, and therefore the different electron-stopping power, across the replica.

In making replicas of aluminum, the surface of the specimen is electrolytically oxidized (anodized), and the oxide film removed by dissolving away the metal. Replicas of other metals can be made in this way by first pressing them into the surface of a piece of soft aluminum, then taking a replica of the imprint.

In another method a fairly thick layer of silver is evaporated onto the specimen surface, under vacuum. This layer is then stripped off, and a layer of collodion or polystyrene allowed to set on it. When this second layer is hard, the silver is dissolved away, leaving a positive image of the original specimen. A negative

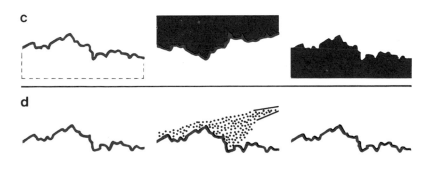

replica can be made by forming the collodion or polystyrene directly on the specimen. If necessary, to improve contrast, and thus make it easier to distinguish features, the replicas can be " shadowed " by evaporating a thin film of metal onto them at a shallow angle.

The Electron-beam Scanning Microanalyser

The last technique to be discussed under the heading of electron-beam/X-ray devices is the electron-beam scanning microanalyser. This combines the electron microscope with the X-ray spectrometer in one piece of equipment, allowing the metallurgist to examine simultaneously both the structure and the composition of minute regions of a metal surface. A fine beam of electrons from an electron microscope tube scans the surface of the specimen over the selected area, and on reflection is used to build up an image on a screen. Simultaneously, characteristic X-rays are produced by the interaction of the electron beam with the metal atoms (in the way we have already seen), thus allowing a pattern to be built up showing the distribution of the elements present. Thus the pictures on page 184 show a structural image formed by a reflected electron beam, and also the distribution of various elements, as light patches. From these the metallurgist can tell, for instance, that the " veins " in the picture on page 184 contain chromium and silicon, but no nickel. The lower pictures show how the instrument can also provide the metallurgist with a graph of the linear distribution of elements in an alloy, in this case the manganese from the upper picture. In the largest of the pictures is the image with the path of a single scan drawn across it. The upper half of the picture shows the linear trace that the apparatus produces when it makes such a scan. Thus in this device we have the most potent method yet for combining structural and compositional analyses of fine details—grain boundaries, precipitation-hardening phases, and so on—and thus for learning more thoroughly than ever before just what gives the alloys their properties.

Ionization Techniques

The remaining group of techniques on page 165 we have classed under the general heading " ionization." In two of them—optical

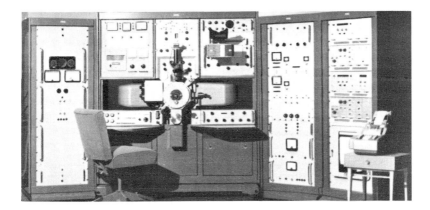

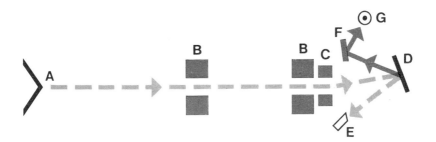

The X-ray scanning microanalyser (photograph at top) solves in one piece of equipment the problem of correlating structure with distribution of constituent elements in metals and alloys. It works on similar principles to an X-ray fluorescence spectrometer, with the vital difference that an electron beam, and not a primary X-ray beam, excites the secondary X-ray emission. In the diagram, (A) is the source of electrons, while (B) and (C) are controlling magnetic fields—an electron microscope, in fact. The electron beam falls onto the specimen surface (D), producing characteristic X-rays (blue line) that are collected and analysed at (F) and (G). The electron beam, meanwhile, is reflected at (D) and forms an image through (E), which measures its intensity. Thus an electron photograph and an X-ray analysis of a single spot can be made simultaneously. By scanning the electron beam over the whole specimen surface a comprehensive picture can be built up.

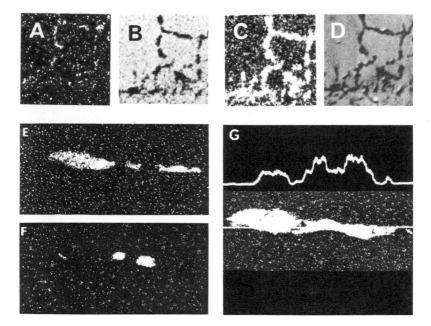

The X-ray scanning microanalyser produces two pictures simultaneously: one electron image (a), which shows up physical details, and one X-ray image (examples b, c, d) showing the distribution of a selected element as light patches. For instance, it can show that the veins in the specimen (a) contain chromium and silicon but no nickel. Pictures (e) and (f) show manganese and sulfur inclusions in steel. Picture (g) shows how the instrument can also provide a graph of the linear distribution of elements in an alloy, in this case the manganese from (f).

spectroscopy and mass spectrography—both of which are methods of compositional analysis, the specimen is ionized in some way, usually by subjecting it to an intense electrical potential. In the first case the resulting light emission is split by a prism or diffraction grating to produce the familiar spectral lines characteristic of the various elements. In the second case the positive ions are accelerated through a powerful magnetic field; the interaction of the field and the ionic charges causes the ions to follow curved paths, the radius of which depends upon the element (in this case the particular isotope involved). By placing a photographic plate (in the mass spectroscope) or scintillation counters (in the mass spectrometer) in the path of the ions, the amounts of each isotope present in the sample can be measured in concentrations as low as one part in 100,000. In the third technique ions from a gas are used to form an image of the surface of a highly charged specimen; alternatively ions from the specimen itself can be used to produce an image, giving a picture of the actual atoms of the specimen, from which their arrangement, faults, etc., can be investigated.

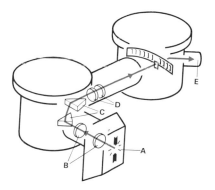

Basic structure of a simple optical spectrometer. The specimen is ionized by electrical discharge (A); light thus produced is focused by lenses (B) and, by passing through a prism system (C), is split into spectrum characteristics of the alloy under examination. Lenses (D) focus this spectrum and pass it on to film strip or an electronic intensity counter through (E).

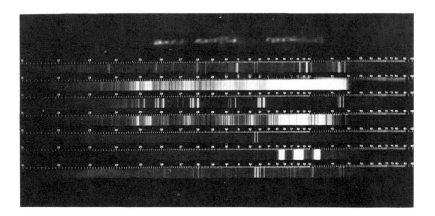

Spectra produced by an optical spectrograph are (top to bottom) for aluminum, tungsten, zinc, iron, copper, carbon, and brass.

The Optical Spectroscope

The optical spectroscope has been used for many years for most kinds of analysis, from simple alloys to the spectra of the stars. Its great virtue to the metallurgist is that it is a rapid technique that can give answers to questions from the furnaceman about his melt in under half an hour, especially if he is only interested in knowing the level of one or two elements in his sample. For many years the spectroscope was also used as a rapid yet accurate technique for research analysis, but today it is being superseded by X-ray analysis, especially where more complex alloys, ores, and so on, are to be analysed.

The Mass Spectrograph

Since its introduction before World War I, the mass spectrograph (joint name for the mass spectroscope and the mass spectrometer) has been put to a very great number of different uses by research scientists. In some industries it is even used for on-line production control. It is not widely used in metallurgy, however, except in research laboratories working on complex alloys where, in particular, the rapid detection of trace elements is essential—in the development of Superalloys for instance. But, like the optical spectrograph, the mass spectrograph has to suffer intense competition from rapidly developing X-ray techniques.

One of the several ways of producing the ion stream in a mass spectrograph is to apply a very high electrostatic charge to the specimen, so that atoms at the surface ionize and are then forced away toward the film of counters by the negative electric field. It is not often used, but it is important to mention it here because the idea leads directly to the final instrument we have to mention, the field-ion microscope, diagramed on page 187.

The Field-Ion Microscope

This device, although not yet perfected, goes far beyond the limits of the electron microscope, allowing the metallurgist to " see " individual atoms, and thus to examine defects on an atomic scale. Ions leaving the surface of the specimen, which must be pointed to give a sufficiently high charge concentration, travel in straight lines to a fluorescent screen and recording system where

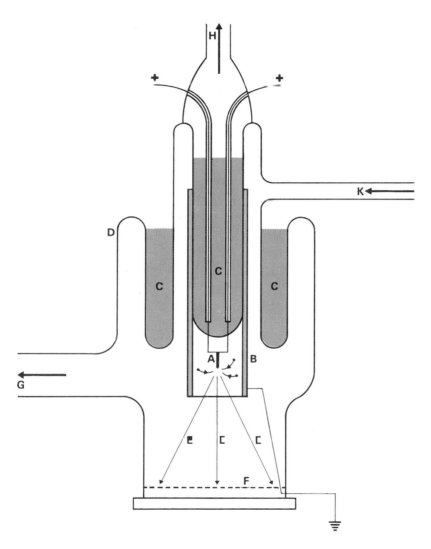

Working diagram of a field-ion microscope, showing fine tungsten wire specimen carrying a high positive charge of static electricity (A), earthed copper cylinder (B), liquid nitrogen coolant (C), Dewar system (D), positive helium ion paths (E), fluorescent screen (F), pipes to and from vacuum pumps (G, H), and supply of low-pressure helium gas (K).

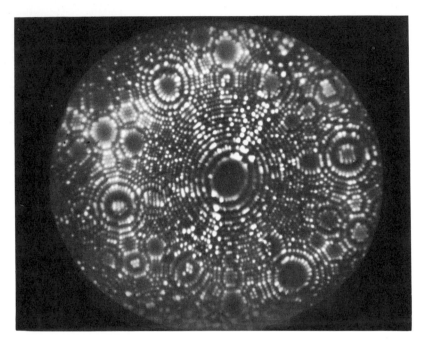

Field-ion microscope photograph of the tip of a tungsten wire. The scintillation spots represent individual atoms.

they form an image of the surface they have just left, each scintillation trace on the screen representing an atomic site. In most versions of the microscope the source of ions is not the specimen itself, but a gas such as helium, neon, or hydrogen. This gets around the obvious difficulty that if the specimen ions are used, the sample surface is changing continuously (although with suitable development this may give us a technique for examining specimens in three dimensions). By applying a voltage below that needed to ionize the metal but above that needed to ionize the low-pressure gas, a stream of ions is obtained without destroying the sample. The effect of the electrostatic field is such that only those coming within a very short distance of the surface and actually associating themselves with a particular atom are ionized, and thus the image formed does show the atomic arrangement and is not simply a picture of random ionizations.

There are still many difficulties to be overcome before the field ion microscope is a fully practical tool. When it is, however, the metallurgist—and other scientists too—will have acquired by far the most potent method yet of investigating solid structures, especially if the possibilities for continuous observation of a changing surface can be fully developed. If that happens, then, for the first time, the metallurgist will really be able to see his subject in three dimensions.

Metallurgy has changed a great deal in the last century, from being one of the most ancient crafts to a modern, and very essential, industrial technology. This book has tried to give some idea of the scope and nature of that change, while at the same time showing that metallurgy is moving on, and in what direction. In describing techniques and theories, we have tried to show trends. In many areas, metallurgy is growing out of itself; the study of advanced alloys merges with other materials sciences, to form one general materials science; fabrication techniques become progressively less and less like traditional metallurgical methods, while these in turn are used increasingly for the fabrication of other materials, particularly the plastics; metallographic and analytical techniques are now no different from the techniques of, say, geology, or even biology; the production of metals becomes more and more like a branch of chemical engineering, and a traffic engineer would probably not feel too far out of his depth running a modern steelworks, or vice versa. All this is perhaps symptomatic of the general trends of modern science and technology in which, more and more each year, the disciplines overlap, merge, and gradually give birth to new kinds of specialists. Nevertheless, for a very long time to come, metals will provide one of the main technical foundations of modern industry, and the metallurgist will remain an individual, if somewhat blurred, entity.

Index

Note: Numbers in italics refer to illustrations and captions to illustrations.

ade.

metals.   +